WHAT IS SALVATION?

WHAT IS SALVATION?

by

E. S. WATERHOUSE, D.D.

*Professor of the Philosophy of Religion
in the University of London*

*With a contribution from the
Biblical standpoint by*

J. W. WATERHOUSE, B.D.

Assistant Lecturer at Didsbury College, Manchester

LONDON
HODDER & STOUGHTON, LIMITED

First published, **1932**

Made and Printed in Great Britain for Hodder & Stoughton, Limited,
by C. Tinling & Co., Ltd., Liverpool, London and Prescot.

THE WESTMINSTER BOOKS
EDITORS' PREFACE

THE general name " THE WESTMINSTER
BOOKS " has been given to this series
of volumes because the original pro-
posal for such a series was made at
a small Committee which met under the
shadow of Westminster Abbey. It will
be noticed that each volume in the series
has a title in the form of a question (" Is
Sin Our Fault ? " " Do Dead Men Live
Again ? " and so on). There is a reason
for this. We live in a time when many
things are being questioned, and notably
religious beliefs and traditional theological
dogmas. The volumes in this series
deal with some of these questions of
ethics and religion which are arousing
interest or causing perplexity to-day in
the minds of many. They are not
academic problems which are here dis-
cussed, but living problems, the kind of
problems which men come up against
every day as they move about in a world
flooded with new knowledge in every

5

department of enquiry. This age, and especially perhaps the younger generation in this age, wants to know what it can really believe about God, the soul, immortality, moral standards and the like, in face of all that is being said by natural science, psychology, comparative religion and Biblical criticism. It is hoped that these books may do something to meet this need. They are written as far as possible without technical language ; they endeavour to look facts fairly in the face, and to shirk no difficulties. The writers belong both to the Church of England and the Free Churches. The series therefore is not the product of any narrow school of thought. The editors have left each author free to state his own opinion, and accept no responsibility for the views expressed. Their work has been mainly that of selecting the authors and securing, so far as is possible, that their contributions do not overlap. It is their confident hope that the series will command a wide attention and be of real help to many in their search for truth.

VERNON F. STORR.
SYDNEY CAVE.

6

CONTENTS

7

CONTENTS

FOREWORD

FOREWORD

The fact that the standpoint of this book is that of psychological enquiry, may explain, and one hopes, excuse, the reversal of the logical order of treatment which would have been to have preceded the psychological investigation by a historical survey of the matter.

Two reasons have led to the course taken. One is that the historical aspect has often and extensively been explored. The other is the wish to focus attention from the first on the actual fact of salvation itself, and its connection, as psychology finds it, with the life and death of Jesus Christ. It is hoped that there will thus result a keener interest in the historical questions involved, if they are approached not abstractly, but as a sequel to our attempt to see what salvation means for us to-day. It may be that the psychology of the matter may illumine the history, as well as the history, the psychology.

I owe to my son, Rev. J. W. Waterhouse, who is much better qualified than I am to deal with the Biblical side of the matter, the whole of the section (Chs. 8 and 9) which deals with that aspect, a section which is essential to any attempt to ask " What is Salvation ? " I also am indebted to him for many suggestions and emendations in what I have written, and for a careful co-operation in the book as a whole.

The last chapter is directed towards a practical outcome of what has been written by us both, and if any such result were made more realisable by what is set forth tentatively here, I should be glad indeed.

E. S. WATERHOUSE.

Richmond College,
University of London.

I
THE PROBLEM

WE cannot remember when we learned to speak of Christ as Saviour. We have done so since our childhood. Yet if we were asked exactly what we meant by the hallowed word, whether we are " saved " and, if so, what precisely has salvation meant to us, how should we answer? There is a theology that every ordinary Englishman somehow acquires which would cause him to say rather vaguely that Christ died for us, and because of that, we are saved by Him. Yet a moment's thought would convince us how many and how varied are the questions that could follow from even so broad and general a statement as that. From what are we saved? How are we saved? Who is, or who is not saved? Is it faith that saves us, and, if so, what place must be given to goodness of life and character? All these and a score more are questions that lie close around the subject. But who is to answer them ?

It is well known that a long history lies behind all this, not only that of the two thousand years since the death of Jesus, but that of more than a thousand years before, the period covered by our Old Testament. It is also true that whatever has a history must be approached through the avenue of that history. Yet this need not be the sole way of approach. The problems surrounding the question of salvation have usually been treated with the assumption, sometimes wittingly, sometimes unwittingly made, that the writers of the New Testament must have possessed a better understanding of them than we can hope to attain. The older idea of inspiration formed a natural basis for this notion. That basis has crumbled, but the notion lingers in most studies of that great event we call the Atonement. Yet is there any sufficient reason why this should be so ?

It is not suggested that we should neglect the Biblical side of the matter. In the present book, a section follows expressly dealing with it, but instead of starting from that point of view, the path chosen here breaks away in another direction. When it has been followed throughout, we shall turn aside to see how far our modern way of approach runs parallel with the Biblical way.

If any justification of this is needed, let us remember that Jesus said but little concerning the manner in which salvation was to be brought to man, though He spoke very definitely concerning the fact that it was at hand. Moreover, the disciples, as the evangelists record, misunderstood what He did say. That what He said is of the utmost significance in approaching the question, all will admit who realize the spiritual insight of Jesus. But it does not follow that the earlier ideas of salvation, which were not expressly connected with what He said, are necessarily more significant

17

B

than anything that may now be said about the matter.

St. Paul and the author to the Hebrews, for example, approached the question from the standpoint of rabbinic lore, rather than directly from the words of Jesus Himself. It was impossible for them to separate the question from the vast sacrificial system which had been so prominently before their eyes from youth upwards. The analogies of priest and victim were, from that point of view, unescapable. They served the purpose of the age, but now they perplex rather than help us. Moreover, in any case, they were the expressions of the theology rather than the preaching of the church. The recorded sermons of the Acts serve to suggest that the resurrection, not the death of Jesus, was the fact most emphasized in apostolic preaching.

After New Testament times, analogies drawn from law became more in evidence, and proved more than ever misleading. The Hebrew notion of God the Sovereign was more to men's minds than the Galilean teaching of the Father in Heaven. As Professor Whitehead has said :

" When the western world accepted Christianity, Cæsar conquered ; and the received text of Western theology was edited by his lawyers. The code of Justinian and the theology of Justinian are two volumes expressing one movement of the human spirit. The brief Galilean vision of humility flickered throughout the ages, uncertainly. In the official formulation of the religion it has assumed the trivial form of the mere attribution to the Jews that they cherished a misconception about their Messiah. But the deeper idolatry, of the fashioning of God in the image of the Egyptian, Persian, and Roman imperial rulers, was retained. The Church gave unto God the attributes which belonged exclusively to Cæsar."

(*Process and Reality*, pp. 484-485.)

Few things have had worse influence on theology than this rendering unto God the things of Cæsar, and the idea of Christ as a hostage, a victim substituted to placate the claim of law for the condemnation of men, arose directly from it.

The indecisive nature of centuries of thought upon the whole subject, and the unsatisfactory character of theories of the Atonement have led to a modern reaction, in which the issue tends to be neglected. This cannot be justified, if we are to have any consideration for the importance of the testimony of the New Testament, and the history of the Christian gospel, in both of which it is revealed as a factor set deep in the Christian experience. We may express doubt as to the relevance of early Christian theology for our purpose of reopening the question, but the relevance of the experience of the early church is not to be gainsaid. In that experience abundant witness is borne to the saving power of Christ and we find that this power was invariably connected with the death on the Cross.

Here, at any rate, we have firm ground for the basis of our enquiry. Psychological investigation need not, any more than legal investigation, consider itself bound to accept the testimony of first-hand witness, but both alike will start by investigating it. That is why our earliest task, as we approach the question " What is Salvation ? " will be to enquire why before any theology existed to connect the death of Christ with the Christian experience of forgiveness of sins, did those who experienced the sense of forgiveness regard the death of Jesus, which came at first as the end of all hope, as the ground of their experience.

The matter, looked at from this viewpoint, resolves itself into a clear issue. Granted that theological explanations of the connection between the death of Jesus and the Christian experience grew up, and one and all proved unsatisfactory, yet that is no reason for ignoring a fact that is abundantly witnessed by history, namely that the death of Jesus was, from the earliest times, connected with the experience of salvation. Let us forget the explanations and start with the fact.

*From the Standpoint
of Psychology*

II

WHAT CHRIST'S DEATH
HAS DONE

WHAT CHRIST'S DEATH HAS DONE

WE have, at any rate, found the point from which our enquiry must start. It is the Cross. As our thought turns to the death of Jesus, we cannot avoid the question—Why did He die? Yet no answer has ever ended the perplexity that the story of the Cross raises in our hearts. Perhaps we are not intended to know. The unsolved mystery lures one to think and think again. What is once answered ceases to be a living issue. Our quest will not be satisfied. Yet the quest may be its own reward apart from any result. The spirit that seeks for results and ceases to seek when it ceases to find, is utilitarian, but singularly unheroic. The " call of the wild," the fascination of the unknowable, the spirit that seeks asking no guarantees, are the marks that distinguish those who mount up with wings like eagles, from the plodding pedestrian spirit of the safety seeker, padding contentedly along the broad paved and lighted highway. To answer such a call Drake went round the Horn and Columbus thrust westward, and their successors still lay their bones to rot in the sun-smitten swamps of the equator, or to freeze amidst the everlasting snows. If on such unguaranteed quests the brave still fare forth, it is a poor prudence on our part to refuse to face a question which we cannot answer. Shall we not at least be better for having asked, whether we find or fail ?

We need not tread the path of former explorers. Our standpoint is to be that of psychology, not theology, and does not embrace such terms as propitiation, substitution, and vicarious sacrifice. Psychology is a descriptive science, and as we look at recorded facts from the psychological standpoint, two questions stand out at once. It is to these that we must turn.

The first question is what was the attitude of Jesus to His own death? One may admit at once that such a question has no meaning if we assume that His death was like that of the martyr, inflicted upon Him by an outside power against His will. No careful reading of the gospels, however, can justify any such assumption. This point is developed in the New Testament survey in Chapter ix. It appears that during His later ministry, Jesus realized His death would be the inevitable issue of a course deliberately adopted. He regarded it as part of His mission in proclaiming the Kingdom, and establishing a new relationship between God and man. It is also evident that He might have avoided arrest by remaining in Galilee, and had He given Pilate such answers as Pilate obviously wanted Him to give, He would have been released by him. It is therefore clear that Jesus foresaw and did not try to avoid the impending doom, regarding it as essential to the purpose of His life, and we can ask what indications are given of the grounds upon which Jesus came to this conclusion, or in other words what He hoped to do by His death.

The second question is even more a matter of fact. Whatever we may think Jesus intended to do, it is undeniable that His death has had a profound effect on the after-course of history. We may ask, therefore, what His death has done, what has been its influence on human life.

If we find that the death of Jesus has done what it seems He intended it to do, we shall get as near as is possible to the answer to the question Why did Jesus die ?—at least from the human side. We shall not attempt to ask more. Theology may need to seek some answer in the nature of God, but from the human side, which is the province of psychology, the intention and result are alone significant.

Turning now to the first of our two questions, it can hardly be doubted from a dispassionate reading of the New Testament that Jesus regarded His death as a necessary part of the service He had come to earth to render, that is to put men into a new and a right relation to God. He did not regard that relation as something easily attained. Yet, on the other hand, the parables of St. Luke xv suggest that Jesus did not consider the obstacle to be on God's side. It lies in man's sin, or, if a non-theological expression is to be found, we may say that man is at " cross purposes " with God because he is out of adjustment with God's purpose for the race as well as for the individual. Jesus taught that a new adjustment was possible, and He connected His death with that new relationship. One cannot say Jesus taught that His death alone was the way of reconciliation. He seems to have regarded it as part of the purpose of His life, and the exclusive attention theology has paid to the death of Jesus as the Atonement gets little support from His own words. It remains, however, that Jesus did think of His death in connection with His life's purpose.

Nowhere did Jesus call His death a condition of divine forgiveness. Only one condition is recorded, that we forgive others. Jesus did not connect either His life or death specifically with forgiveness. He assumed God was ready to forgive, if we forgave. It is not the teaching of Jesus, therefore, that has connected the death on the Cross with God's act of forgiveness, but rather that of the Epistles, which lie outside the scope of our treatment here.

If, however, God forgives, that means His own resentment against the evil doer is laid aside, but there still remains the wrong, its influence and example. It is the future of what is wrong that is untouched by the forgiveness that overlooks the past. Most theories of the Atonement have utterly neglected that future, except in so far as to say that pardon involves that no future consequences shall react on the offender. None the less when the sinner is forgiven, his sin remains, and this aspect has been strangely neglected.

Happily, we think less at the present time of those explanations of the death of Christ which regard it as a punishment. The civilised world has yet to make up its mind as to what it intends to achieve by punishment. If it be said that punishment restrains evil, all that can be claimed is that the world would be much worse if there were none, for we have never yet succeeded thereby in eliminating crime. In days when penalties were far more severe than now there was proportionately more crime, which suggests that other things than punishment have worked such improvement as there is. Punishment deals with a symptom, not with the cause of wrong. It put nothing right, and therefore cannot have been the reason for the Cross.

When sin has been committed, whether forgiveness follows or not, the past remains ; what we *can* alter is the future. It is noteworthy that the chief reference to His death made by Jesus was to call it a ransom. The metaphor can hardly have been adopted carelessly, and two Synoptists record it. The words admit of more than one interpretation, but the metaphor suggests the release of a captive from the power that holds him. It refers to the future still to be determined, not to the past that is irrevocable. If then we think of the death of Christ not in terms of punishment or even as the substitution of one for another, but rather as a means of freeing man from the power that holds him, we are supported by the chief reference He made to His own end.

From the psychological point of view, this is most significant, because every student of Christian experience is struck by the number of times that those who have passed through the experience of a sense of pardon have connected it with the death of Christ. It does not seem sufficient to explain this by saying that they have been taught so to associate it. No theological dogma unsupported by experience could have found so wide a confirmation. In some way or other the death of Jesus has been connected with the sense of pardon in the lives of millions.

From the psychological standpoint, therefore, we ask what that connection may be. In doing so it is essential to forget for a while all the theological explanations of the link between Christ's death and sin. That does not imply that they are rejected as false without a hearing. Though all cannot be true, some may be. Yet, if once we approach a matter with a preconceived notion of what we shall find there, it is a psychological commonplace that we shall

c

find what we look for, and nothing else. We must endeavour, therefore, to seek in the experience of those who are " saved," a reason for that state of mind which is to them the sign of salvation. One cannot believe that anyone would accept the statement that he was now " saved " unless there was some confirmatory change in his own experience. Theologically, salvation implies the act of God, but psychology as a descriptive science is limited to studying salvation in the attitude of man. The psychological question before us, therefore, is What effect has the death of Jesus had upon the minds of men who have been given a changed attitude towards life, and, especially, towards their own sense of wrongdoing?

The primary answer is that the death of Christ has opened men's eyes to the character of sin. It is our habit to think of abstract qualities by means of actual instances; of honesty, for

34

example, by means of honest actions. Similarly, it may have been the actual sin and treachery that compassed the death of Christ, rather than sin in general, which first struck the imagination when the death of Christ was remembered in Christian preaching. The Pharisee, Pilate and Judas have certainly had their share of the world's execration, and the story of the Best and Greatest being hounded to death by cruelty and treachery struck home in a way that no warning against sin in general could ever have done. The story of the Cross showed the world that sin kills goodness, and awoke in man a sense of shame and horror that nothing else could have aroused. It is quite in keeping with the laws of the working of our minds that the lesson of the Cross should exert an influence far greater than the preaching of the prophets or the warnings of the moralists.

The story of Calvary has for ever swept away the light and superficial view of the nature of wrong that characterised the Greeks. It has fixed on the mind and conscience of the Gentile world something of the Hebrew gravity of outlook regarding sin. In so doing, it has worked towards that release from the bondage of evil which is the essence of salvation. If the Greek idea that sin was ignorance is in any way right, those who do wrong are always in ignorance as to the full character of wrong-doing. The death of Jesus more than any other happening in history has removed this ignorance.

Yet again, it has often been suggested that the Atonement should be spelt at-one-ment for it implies the unifying of God and man. The death of Jesus has proved the way. As Dr. Glover has put it, suffering is a *lingua franca* that all comprehend. " I could die for you " is the lover's litany, and Calvary has been the fount of love, for it has shown that God's love is even unto death. It is psychologically

36

true that the approach through the emotions is by far the surest way in which truth enters and is enshrined in the heart. The great Islamic schism between Sunni and Shiah is fostered by the pathos of the death of Hussein and the belief that his death in battle was a veritable martyrdom. Legend and history join to show how potent is the appeal of self-sacrificial suffering. The teaching of Jesus, apart from His death, would have been incomplete. Love is not created by anything except emotion. We admire Plato. We do not say we love him. It is impossible to love a man because his words are wise and good. The words of Jesus without the love of Jesus would have a far less effect upon mankind. If Jesus had died in ripe old age He would have remained incomparably the greatest teacher of all time, but He would not have been the object of the world's adoration. To imagine that the teaching of Jesus may be separated from His

life and, still more, from His death,
is an utter misreading of the nature of
mankind. We are familiar from childhood with the words " Thou shalt love
the Lord thy God," but we seldom ask
what is meant by love that is com-
manded. To say that we must love
is to ask for an impossibility. One
imagines that in those lands where parents
arrange their children's marriages, they
may tell the pair that they must marry
one another, but they cannot make
them love each other. To love a God,
who is not known to love us, is an
impossibility. The death of Jesus has
fixed itself upon the world's imagination
as the sign and seal of the love of God,
and, therefore, has enabled men to love
God in a way otherwise impossible.
The God who loves me demands what
the Maker and Lord cannot evoke.
Only once did Jesus refer to His Father
as Lord of Heaven and Earth. Love
is the fulfilling of the law, and when
man loves God, the fulfilling of His

law is made possible. The fulfilling of God's law means the separation from sin. Once again the death of Christ brings mankind out of the power of evil, " a ransom for many."

On the psychological side, therefore, the death of Christ serves actually to deliver man from the power of his own wrongdoing by awakening him to its nature, and by creating a sense of love towards God, whose love is revealed in the Cross. That the words " God so loved the world, that He gave," are amongst the most well beloved in Scripture is proof enough of the connection between redemptive love and the life and death of Jesus, for words that awoke no echoes in the experience of men could never have had the response that has been given to these.

If from the theological side it is objected that nothing has been said here of any change in the divine attitude, the reply is that this must necessarily lie beyond our scope, which is concerned with observable facts. Chief amongst these is that the death of Christ, by reason of the two points we have stressed, if for none other, has a connection with the awakening of man to a sense of his sin, and also with the awakening of man to believe in the love of God, with all the appeal that love makes. It is also clear that nothing else has served the same purpose in any similar way.

We are still far from answering the question "Why did Jesus die?" and no full answer is likely to be found, but from the psychological standpoint we can at least connect the death of Christ with that changed attitude of men towards evil which is, at any rate, the outward mark of being "saved." Owing to theological difficulties it has often been declared that the death of Jesus was in no sense an atonement, but merely the seal on a life of self-sacrifice. That question is not before us, but we can at any rate say that the

death of Jesus has had an effect that
no other death has ever had and that
it has produced a vast change in millions
of lives. If the death of Jesus was as
the death of the other prophets, there
is no explanation of the fact that it
has moved men as their deaths did not.
How many, for example, could even
name the prophet who was slain between
the Temple and the Altar? Yet, no
doubt, he was a just man martyred
for his zeal for truth. Even if it be
said that Jesus was the greatest of the
prophets, there is no reason in that
for the unparalleled effect that His death
has wrought compared with theirs. Psychology is not concerned with any reasons
which are used for or against connecting
the death of Christ with the forgiveness
of sin, but any student of the psychology
of religion must admit that there is a
great and vital connection between the
belief in Christ's death as a deliverance
from sin and that deliverance itself,
for there is nothing whatever that in

any comparable degree has changed men's lives and liberated them from evil, as has their belief in the saving power of the Cross. We must, therefore, admit that in fact the death of Jesus does save. It is still possible, of course, to argue that there is no actual connection between that death and salvation, just as there may be no connection save the faith of the patient between the medicine and the result it is supposed to perform, but, even so, faith healing is a matter for psychological study. How much more then the fact of salvation ?

Whatever, therefore, be the theological difficulties of connecting the death of Christ with the salvation of man, the connection in experience, which is the subject matter of a psychological study, is clear. Indeed, one is inclined to think that theory has here suggested difficulties to obscure what is so obvious in practice that it would be accepted without question were it not for pre-conceived notions of sin and the Godhead.

Few of those difficulties are serious. To ask whether God could not have found another way is an inadmissible question since it demands for an answer a knowledge of the Divine will which no one can hope to possess. One might as well ask why God created a world at all, and allowed evil therein. Nor does it seem to the point to object that if Christ's death were in any sense connected with sin He had not committed, it was unjust. If so, life is unjust from beginning to end. Often others must unwillingly bear the consequences of sin not their own. But where one willingly suffers for another, we see the highest characteristics of humanity —" Greater love hath no man than this." Moreover, it is a law of heroism that if the strong can suffer for the weak, they shall not refuse to take the strong man's burden. It is not "just" that a man shall lose his life in a vain attempt to pull some wretched suicide from the river; it is something *more* than just. Justice holds scales of reckoning in her hands, but the finest things of life pass all reckoning. Admit, if you will, that if Jesus died for sins not His own it was " unjust." It yet remains that there is that which is far more than justice.

Those objections which deal with the supposed effect upon God of the death of Christ do not come before us because we are not concerned with either denying or affirming the connection between God's attitude to sin and Christ's death. All we have insisted upon is that there is a connection in fact between the belief in the power of Christ, a power exercised through His death most of all, and a changed attitude on man's part to life and sin.

It is this change that constitutes the " Atonement," as psychology views it. If we use the word in these pages it bears from henceforth that connotation. The objection may be raised that this is to declare for a purely manward

44

view of the Atonement. The reply is that for psychology this is the only side that can be considered. What else there may be to be said must be left to theology.

From the standpoint we take here, therefore, the influence of Jesus, an influence created by His life and teaching, and culminating in the death that has so profoundly stirred the conscience of the world, has the power of changing human lives. The Atonement, in the psychological sense, is a fact. Though even a complete psychological explanation of the way in which the life and death of Christ affect men's lives is wanting, we do not therefore deny their power. Just in the same way we do not deny the fact of hypnosis nor the evidence for occasional " telepathic " intercommunication, though in the former case, little is known of the manner in which a hypnotic state arises, and in the latter, practically nothing of the conditions of " telepathy." Respect for facts of experience prevents us denying what we cannot explain, if the evidence of such happenings is sufficient. The evidence for an actual connection between the life and death of Christ and salvation is so vast as to be unchallengeable. It is impossible to think that if it were an accepted fact that the death of Christ had no connection with man's salvation, Christianity would continue to produce transformed lives. We approach our investigation of the question "What is Salvation" by asserting the fact that salvation follows belief in Him in millions of instances. Our next task will be to see how, as a matter of fact, the new life in Christ is lived. Salvation is not a closed mystery on every side. The man who is saved exhibits certain signs of the change. It is for us to ask what these are and how they are manifested.

*From the Standpoint
of Psychology*

III

THE TRANSFORMATION
OF LIFE

THE TRANSFORMATION OF LIFE

SO far we have been occupied in considering how we are to understand the persistent belief of mankind which connects salvation with the death of Christ. With regard to this particular question, our standpoint was psychological, and it differs from the theological in that theology seeks to "justify the ways of God to man," whilst psychology is content to describe them empirically. If now we go a step further and ask what we mean when we speak of anyone being "saved," we shall still occupy the same standpoint and be restricted to enquiring what difference in behaviour is manifested in the "saved" man. This is because psychology as a descriptive science is limited to the study of behaviour, though this need not carry the assumption of an extreme American school, the Behaviourists, that only outward activity,

D

and not mind, is a subject for psychology. If behaviour is not a manifestation of mind, it is difficult to say what it can be. Our concern is with behaviour manifest in actions and speech, but we shall make our inferences none the less as regards the mind behind it. When we ask, then, what are the distinguishing marks of the man who has experienced salvation, we find that salvation is often taken to be the same as the forgiveness of sins. Yet at the same time, evangelical tradition emphasises the fact that repentance and faith are its prerequisites. If salvation, as many seem to think, is simply a term interchangeable with pardon, these prerequisites do not find support in the teaching of Jesus, which is quite definite in saying that the condition of forgiveness is that we forgive others, and that the unforgiven are the unforgiving. We must be prepared, therefore, to regard salvation as wider than forgiveness, and indeed, popular opinion, as well as theology, demands that faith must prove itself in works, and that those who are saved must show the quality of their salvation in their lives. Yet this introduces a question that is very seldom faced, rarely indeed asked —If salvation be a religious issue, why insist that it must be shown in compliance with certain moral standards ?

Common consent demands that the man who claims to be saved shall witness to that fact by strict compliance with a certain accepted moral code. If we hear that he has been fined for travelling without a ticket or adulterating butter, we express doubt as to the sincerity of his religious profession. Yet precisely what is the connection between religion as the sense of the higher power at work in the universe and such a mundane matter as the adulteration of butter ? One can quite understand why socially it is undesirable that food stuffs should be adulterated, but why introduce religion into social necessity ?

Someone may reply that he would not give much for the religion of a man who had so poor a conscience. Exactly, but in that case if a man is an admirable example of what society approve, and at the same time be a firm sceptic, would the experience of salvation add anything to his good qualities ? If it would not, is it a superfluity ? If religion is to be identified with morals, why not call it morality at once ? Why make a difference ? If it is not, why be so doubtful as to the religion of the man whose moral life shows some defects ?

For example, a man said once in my hearing that his idea of the religious man was the man who carried out the gospel of St. Matthew's twenty-fifth chapter, and that if he did so, nothing else mattered. I told him I knew a man who spent his whole life in attending to the needs of the poor and relieving them, and yet that man went to no place of worship, and as far as I knew, had no special religious beliefs. My companion hailed this with enthusiasm, and said we needed more of this sort and "less psalm-singers." I replied that there were quite a number like the man in question, as he was the relieving officer! My companion was not at all pleased, and indeed was unkind enough to call my reply a "quibble," though I pointed out that the relieving officer did exactly the kind of work which he declared was the sole task of religion. His attitude, however, made it clearer than ever to me why Socrates was put to death!

Such an illustration, however, serves to show how shallow it is to identify religion with charitable conduct, apart altogether from the motive. I take it that the keenest supporter of the view that those who contribute to the welfare of their fellow men are the best example of religion, would exempt the type of service that does unhappily sometimes occur, when a man will endow

a hospital with a view to a knighthood.
He relieves much suffering, it is true,
but the self-seeking aim, as all agree,
removes his action from the category
of acts of moral merit. If then we
are agreed that there must be some
sign in a man's life to prove the reality
of the experience of salvation, and if
we expect this sign to be given in his
moral conduct, we must ask the question
too seldom asked, What is the precise
relation between religion and morality ?
It is impracticable to identify religion
with even the highest morality, for if
so, we must classify amongst the religious
some eminent sceptics who would object
strongly to our doing so. Yet we cannot
classify as religious those whose moral
code is wrong. What is then the precise
relation between the two ?

We are so familiar with the close
connection of religious belief and moral
action that it may seem strange if we
say that probably in their origin religion
and morals sprang from separate roots.

Yet the likeliest object of the earliest religious feelings was what Otto has labelled for us the " Numinous," and there is nothing definitely moral or rational about the Numinous. The primitive attitude towards it is one of awe, which much more truly than fear, should be called the early religious emotion. Awe is a compound of wonder, fear and self-abasement, and the unfamiliar and portentous is always a source of awe. Man's primitive religious attitude was centred upon the Numinous, not specially connected with his tribal moral code, and in so far as it was related to the Numinous, had no special moral significance.

Morality, on the other hand, seems to be based at root on that inner sense of discrimination between the things that must and must not be done, which all creatures, even the higher animals, exhibit in their social life. This is not to say that there is a definite moral instinct or intuition, but to point out that instincts of the group or herd exhibit preferential characteristics towards certain types of action, and that even the wolf pack will punish its members who transgress its peculiar laws. Man would be a strange creature if he had no such sense, and the earliest law of conduct was " Thou shalt follow the way of the tribe and not introduce thine own innovations therein." Where then is the link between the awe-inspiring Numinous, the primitive fount of religion, and the rule of the tribe, from which moral precepts developed ?

It is not far to seek. The Numinous was a matter of concern just in so far as it was believed to have effect on the affairs of the tribe. That it was held to enter into their life in manifold ways for good or bad is indubitable. Hence it became all important that the Numinous should be rightly approached. It must not be enterprised or taken in hand lightly, unadvisedly or wantonly. No man takes the office

of priest, "shaman," medicine man or
whatever it is, to himself, without strict
training and subjection to many "tabus."
It is for him to approach the Numinous
on behalf of the tribe, and to find the
right way of approach. Early peoples
were very conscious of the solidarity
of their social group for weal or woe.
Even to Joshua, it seemed perfectly
natural that Israel should be defeated
because a single individual had secretly
broken a "tabu," and not only Achan,
but all his family and possessions, had
to suffer to wipe out the crime.

The sole crime of primitive society
is the breach of "tabu," but it is a
very serious crime. Now, not only
are "tabus" the laws of the primitive
folk, but they are regarded as connected
with the god. When once an established
ritual of approach to the Numinous
becomes accepted, and the Numinous is
linked with the tribal god, the "tabus"
which surround it are binding on all,
and, in time, the customs of the tribe

gain sanction from the idea that they represent the law of the tribal god. In that way, though religion and morals spring from separate roots, the two intertwine inseparably from earliest days. Dr. Marett has said that the keeping of " tabu " was the seed bed of personal religion. A man may be conscious that though a " tabu " has been violated, and perhaps the tribe has suffered, he has not been the guilty party. Presently the guilty one, or he who is assumed to be guilty, which to primitive peoples is the same thing (as it is to a modern mob), is discovered and punished. The man who has kept the " tabu " cannot avoid a feeling of pride that his hands are clean. He distinguishes himself from the sinner who has violated " tabu." That is to say, there dawns on him the sense of a relationship to the god different from the relationship of others in the tribe—the seed of a personal religion.

All this may seem a long way

from our subject, but it is more germane than is superficially apparent. It explains why society requires a moral test for religious belief, and what is more, it explains why certain people have a religious sense, and very little of the conventional moral code of their day.

The religious sense still relates primarily to the Numinous, the mysterious side of the universe. Poets, artists and seers must possess it. There never yet was a great poet without this sense of the Numinous, but there have been not a few poets whose lives have scandalized their day and generation. We do not have a compulsory moral code for poets, and so these men have not been denied the name of poet because of their moral failings. Yet we fail to see that the same reason explains why certain men have had a religious side to their lives and nevertheless have lapsed badly in the moral sphere. If we recollect that the Numinous and the moral are distinct at root, we shall no longer be puzzled by the occasional conflicts between the two in certain cases.

This explains why a man like Oscar Wilde may be more capable of a spiritual outlook on life than many conventionally moral people. It does not excuse the moral lapses such men exhibit, but a clearer understanding of the spiritual sense, and the moral sense, will prevent the uncharitable judgment that a man who has shown spiritual interests and fails morally must have inevitably have been a hypocrite in regard to the former.

We can now return to our original point. What is the differentia of the saved man? We have seen why the change that we expect should be found in moral relationships, and why it is not true that moral relationships even of the most unexceptionable character are the same as religion. Yet the sense of the Numinous, for us the sense of the immanence of God in daily life, must mean the transformation of life, and we must now ask what exactly that transformation means.

One does not wish to say anything that seems to make light of a matter which is sacred, yet one cannot resist the uneasy feeling that much of the preaching of evangelicalism has resulted in an impression that to be saved means being put in a mysterious relation to God, through faith in the death of Christ, whereby the believer becomes favoured as one of the inner and elect circle of disciples, assured that all is now well with him. Nearly all religions have an inner and an outer circle. The religion that disputed with Christianity for the supremacy of the Roman world, Mithraism, was decidedly of this type. Christ defeated Mithras,

but Mithraic ideas lingered, as the
Canaanites lingered when nominally
dispossessed by Joshua, in the midst
of the realm of their conqueror.
It is hard to resist the inference that
much high sacramentarian teaching
owes more to Mithraic habits of
thought than to the New Testament,
and in the same way, the desire
to be in the innermost grade was
thoroughly Mithraic, for the religion
Jesus preached cannot be said in
any way to suggest different orders
for the saint, the enthusiast and
average man. We must, at all costs,
rid ourselves of the notion that
salvation is a definite possession,
got once and for all at a definite
crisis or point of time and then
automatically retained.

Ought we not to regard salvation
as a process rather than a fact,
and the saved as " such as were
being saved ? " Psychology certainly
recognizes a difference in life following

upon the experience of salvation, but it seems to be a difference that is made gradually manifest over a lifetime. Its essence is this. All of us are egoists born. Self is the first natural centre of existence. Yet the key saying of Jesus, indeed the only one found in all four Gospels, and five times in the four, declares that those who find their lives lose them. "If any man come after me, let him deny himself." How poorly are those words interpreted if they are taken to refer to some small self-denial! They surely imply that the natural centre of life, self, must be rejected, and that the centre must be thrown outside into something wider. That is the essence of salvation. The unsaved are those who never escape from themselves. To be saved implies the discovery of a new self by finding a new centre. It follows that there are analogies in other spheres. An artist in his devotion to beauty, a scientist in his devotion to truth, a statesman in service for his country, a worker who lives for his work, all show some of the marks of a saved man. No great man ever yet lived for himself. Napoleon was a great man, though few would call him a good man, but he would not have been great if his ambition had been purely personal. It was the vision of a great France that made Napoleon great. He found himself in something more than self.

How seldom is it that one finds the mother of a family a woman little in spirit ! St. Paul speaks of woman as saved " by means of " motherhood, if we are to accept Sir William Ramsay's interpretation of the real meaning of the original. The thought suggested here, one admits, hardly seems Pauline, but one can imagine Jesus saying it. Motherhood is so essentially the unselfish calling that the mother can hardly help losing and therefore finding herself, which is the essence of salvation. How often, on the other hand, do we meet the self-centred old maid and bachelor, who, just because they have never had need to think in any other terms than those of self, have lost themselves. This is not to say that all such must be the restricted personalities which so many are. Those who have had a vocation, and have lived for a cause, have had the moral equivalent of parenthood and gained its advantages, but no self-centred person ever possessed a true personality.

But the chief means of breaking from the old centre and leading to a new one has been the life and death of Jesus. As we have seen, the death of Christ is essential. A recent writer has suggested that love is too readily identified with an emotion, rather is it an act of will.

65

E

He points out that the Samaritan possessed no feeling of affection for the Jew, a natural enemy, whom he succoured, but he had the will to serve. Yet this surely overlooks the important fact that compassion was the emotion in this case. The priest and Levite lacked human pity, and Jesus wished to show that piety was no substitute for pity. Without an emotional stirring, the will acts slowly. Even the ideal of the life of Jesus loses half its power apart from the story of the Cross. It is not that the death of Jesus in an almost magical way acts on man and saves him if he consents to be saved. The death of Jesus wakes man to the fact of the essential wrongness of his life, breaks the stony ground of the heart and rouses the sense of love. Then the story of the life of Jesus makes its appeal, and with the realisation of what He is and means, comes a new

outlook characteristic of the life of
the saved.

Moreover, there is communion with
Christ. It is impossible to deny
the reality of the experience to which
millions have testified. Millions have
found through every type of creed
and in every age for 2,000 years,
the reality of the sense of communion
with Him. In this the average believer
shares with the mystic, and if his
experience is less dazzling and less
manifest, it is none the less indubitable.
Our theology explains it as the
presence of the living, risen Christ.
Psychology is not concerned with the
explanation, but every psychologist
who has studied Christian experience
must recognise the fact. I have often
tried to question it, asking myself
whether it is not due to early training
and sacred associations, but as often
as I suggest this to myself, am I
made to feel that it does not meet
the case. The sense of Christ in

a believer *is* something different. He
has other heroes, yet cannot ever
obtain from contemplation of them
what the thought of Christ brings
to him. He cannot rid himself of
the feeling that the mystic is right,
that even to his more ordinary consciousness there is something of that
communion of which the mystic speaks.
Whether it should be called communion
with God, or with Christ, is a
smaller matter. Only the contemplation
of Christ brings it, as nothing else
does, and it is impossible, therefore,
to deny that the experience has nothing
to do with Him.

Salvation is the taking up of a
man's life into the life of Christ.
It begins when Jesus lays hold
of any man as He laid hold of
Paul. In the case of the apostle,
a cataclysmic spiritual experience began
the process, but the conversion was
a prelude to a life reshaped by
Christ. Salvation is less marked,

68

and its results less epoch-making in ordinary lives than in the life of St. Paul, but at root there is the same experience. A man finds a new centre. In St. Paul's own words, which reflect his own experience, such a man is a " new creation." The spirit and ideals of the Master make their own appeal and he follows after to lay hold of that for which Christ laid hold of him. He begins a new life. It does not follow that it is realized at the time. Often indeed, when a man has made a sudden decision in the sense that he at a given moment definitely pledges himself to the ideal of Christ which has gripped his mind, he wonders that he does not " feel different." He has heard perhaps of those who have experienced ecstatic joy, and is almost disappointed that such is not his. Yet this is in every way a secondary thing, depending largely on the state of mind that preceded the decision, rather than on the decision itself. Those whose decision was preceded by a great struggle of mind, naturally experience a greater sense of relief when it terminates. In part, too, it is temperamental. One notices how differently different men take news that has a great bearing on their future, how an honour or a humiliation excites some, while others remain, outwardly at least, impassive. Yet in both cases alike, however different are the first reactions, the change will be realised as years go by, and it is not otherwise with religious conversion. It is the beginning of a new life, and although at first there may seem no outward difference, when, after a few years, those who have had the experience look back, they are in no doubt as to the magnitude of the change.

Others change but slowly under the spell of Christ. Without sudden crisis or any vivid experience, the old self-centred life begins to yield, like the ice during a slow thaw, and a new life reveals itself. In every case, sudden or slow, the reality of the conversion is manifested by the change in the life. The old controversy of faith or works as the ground of salvation, as was previously suggested, has lost its point. Salvation is neither of faith nor of works alone. A venture of faith calls men to the feet of Christ, but that is the beginning, not the end, of salvation. None the less, it is not the most exact fulfilment of the severest moral code that marks the saved man. Rather is it the re-centreing of life, and the works that follow are the consequence. Salvation is the process by which the spirit of Christ exerts its influence upon the life of man, so as to create a new centre. Normally this involves a conscious acceptance of

the leadership and Lordship of Christ.
Yet there are lives that make no
such acknowledgment, that even reject
the claim of Christ, yet indirectly,
but none the less solely, owing to
His influence, are transformed from
self to service. Are they not saved ?
May they not be the other sheep,
not of this fold ? May we not find
salvation is something far wider than
our thought of it ?

If salvation be the transforming
of life by the spirit of Christ, there
must be degrees of salvation according
as there are degrees of transformation,
and some must be more saved than
others. Salvation is not a talismanic
gift bestowed in the same way and
with similar results in all cases. The
spirit of Jesus ranges over a field
wider than the circle of His avowed
disciples, and may there not be many
saved even by Him they know not ?
It would be a narrow religion, and
surely the religion of Jesus can never

be that, which admitted the dying thief to salvation and left Plato outside.

Must there not also be those amongst the saved whose salvation is indirect and unwitting? They have come under the influence of Christ without knowing it. Their lives, which they think owe nothing to Him, owe all to Him. In the scientific meaning of the term, and not of course in any offensive sense, they are parasitic on Christianity. The parasite is independent of the host from whom it draws sustinence, but if the host perish, so must the parasite. In the same way, there are many who in apparent independence of Christ, live upon what He has provided, and were Christianity to disappear, they would disappear with it.

There may be, therefore, agnostics and others amongst the saved, possibly to their own surprise. " When saw we Thee ? " they will ask, only to

learn that though they never knew
their teacher, inasmuch as they had
learned from Him, they were His
disciples. Out of the darkness of the
self-centred life they had followed, to
lose their Guide in the light of the
life of love and loyalty, but the Guide
was Christ, and they followed, the
sheep who knew not their shepherd.

Perhaps the journey is not yet over.
If salvation be a process rather than
a fact, we must assume that if a
man does not consciously " find salvation " on earth he is lost. The
hereafter may begin where the here
leaves off, and those whose salvation
is partial may need the fulfilment that
the hereafter may bring.

Be that as it may, there is as well
as this indirect, a very direct and well
marked evidence of the reality of the
saving experience in man.

If we have judged rightly, salvation
consists in the awakening of a new
life in man, the ending of the old

self-centred life, and the throwing of
life's centre into something other than
self, in short, losing one's self to find
one's self. The life and death of Jesus
combine to exert the power which,
working upon the heart and conscience
of men, frees them from the past and
gives the heritage of the future.
Salvation is a process, and reaches
backwards and forwards, and it may
even mean that the past is altered.
The miracle is achieved, the unalterable
past is changed. This is best shown
by an actual case, one of many millions.
I once heard a frank and touching
testimony from a man whose past evil
habits had caused him to contract a
painful malady. He said that when
first he realized he was a victim, he
raged like a newly caught wild beast
to the exhaustion point, and then broke
down. His fury altered to sullen bitterness. After a time of suffering, he
found the mercy of the God he had
ignored, and in his new-found joy

expected a speedy cure. He was disappointed. When he realized he was not cured, he understood it as punishment for his past sin, and yet he had experienced the sense of pardon, and it puzzled him that the God who pardoned, should still exact a penalty. At last it was revealed to him that there was no punishment, but like St. Paul's thorn, a cross to carry that the grace of God might be manifested in him. " So," he added, " do I carry it ; now I have lost all bitterness, and all sense of being punished. I know my suffering is the result of my past, but God has changed that past, and it is no longer the cause of a curse, but of a cross that He will make a crown."

The mere fact of the past is unimportant. The only significance of the past is in so far as it is the mortgagee of the future. When that mortgage is paid off, the fact that once it was held is of no importance. Like a cancelled I.O.U. that once was kept carefully and carried full value, it can now be tossed into the fire. The past is changed when its consequences are changed.

This more than anything else is the first characteristic of salvation. Some men who experience a sudden transformation break with the past with startling suddenness. Others struggle slowly. But the beginning of the new life must synchronize with the disappearance of the old, and the saved life frees itself from those parts of the old life which are incompatible with the new ideal. Such is the thought of Wesley's line :

> " He breaks the power of cancelled sin
> He sets the prisoner free."

The sin is " cancelled " by pardon, but the power of the habit of sin remains. The past, however, is changed in its consequences, because the setting up of a new centre in conversion decentres the old, and the usual consequences cease to follow. The saved man becomes the new creation of which St. Paul speaks.

There is a certain interesting correspondence here with the methods of modern psychological treatment. Spinoza anticipated the method of psychoanalysis when he said that an emotion which is a passion ceases to be a passion, when we form a clear and distinct idea of it. Substitute " complex " for passion, and the method is there in a nutshell. It is held that the essence of cure is to bring out the complex from the central position it has secured in the patient's unconscious mind, and then to relate it to his normal consciousness. Then, so to speak, the swelling goes down. It is the same decentralizing process which takes place in conversion.

But still further, psychological therapeutic method leads the patient away from himself and his "fixation," and re-educates him. Strictly speaking, this method does not try to cure the

complex but cuts off its root and leaves
it to subside of itself. Concentration
on the ideal of Christ does exactly the
same thing for the man who is saved.
It takes him away from himself, and
by so doing creates the new self in
him. A couple of cases that have come
lately to my notice will illustrate what
I mean.

The one was that of a young man
who came to me, a prey to morbid
fear. There was probably a childhood
obsession at the root, and when I
explained what this was, he admitted
I was right, though he had not thought
of the experience in that light before.
But the explanation by itself did not
help, and I told him he must find a
new self, for his present self lay at the
root of his trouble. I advised him to
undertake social work in connection
with a mission, and he agreed to do so.
It is now six months since he began,
and the difference is amazing. He has
begun to find himself and what is more,,

to find God ; the sense of God in his life is literally making a new man of him. He still has struggles, and still feels the old trouble at times, but whereas it was fast becoming an obsession, it is now an incident. The complex is dissolving because a new self is forming, and in the new self the complex finds no nourishment. The roots have been cut, and it will wither away.

We still hear a good deal about "too much religion," and the supposed evils that result from over emphasis of the religious side of life in immature minds, but we are not told enough of the troubles which arise through stifling the religious sense. If we live and move and have our being in God, neglect of God means lack of adaptation to spiritual environment and all the corresponding troubles which ensue. I am convinced that there are far more people suffering unhappiness because they have too little religion than because they have too much. Practically every man believes in God, and by the very definition, God is the greatest existent reality. Is it likely then that lives which neglect the greatest of realities will be happy or well balanced? In the case I have just mentioned, the man concerned had no particular interest in religion, and no sooner had I spoken to him than I was convinced that his need more than anything else was a religious experience. I did not tell him so, nor speak especially about religious matters. I was sure that the social service I suggested would be the doorway to a religious awakening, and so it proved to be. He has not experienced any definite " conversion " in the sense of a crisis, or even a sharp realization but the change is at work. The last few months have given unmistakable indications of it. He is finding Christ in the service of Christ.

One must admit that just as psychological treatment has definite limits as regards those who are advanced in

F

years, so religious conversion is seldom experienced in later life. There are exceptions, but in comparison they are few when set side by side with the stirrings of adolescence. Yet the other case, though not a religious conversion, is sufficiently parallel to be quoted as an example of what salvation can mean. Two or three years ago, in some broadcast talks, I spoke about the conquests of fear. One of my listeners was a village blacksmith, who was a Christian man. All his life he had been nervous of horses, and never shod one without more or less trepidation. He said nothing about his fears, for obvious reasons, but the horses knew, as horses would, and they gave him more trouble than other smiths ever got. This strange fear was spoiling his life. It seems ludicrous to tell of a blacksmith afraid of shoeing a horse, yet that state of things was no joke for the unfortunate man condemned to a livelihood that brought a constant fear he dared not reveal. As he listened to the broadcast, it suddenly occurred to him that in God was the power he lacked. God would not fear the creatures He had made. Why not trust God for the power to cast out his fear? He went to work next day with a new determination, and began to face his work in a new spirit. He was not a young man and the fear was long standing, but under the new idea of the power of God it began to lose its ugly features. I have since heard that he is steadily overcoming it and is happier than he had been for many a year. That case is interesting in that it shows how a man past middle life, by realizing the unrealized resources of his own religious faith, can overcome an old and morbid fear, and is another sign of the fulness of meaning in salvation.

From the Standpoint
of Psychology

IV

**THE TRANSFORMATION
OF THOUGHT**

THE TRANSFORMATION
OF THOUGHT

THE kind of history to which most of us were apprenticed at school gave a misleading idea, which many have never unlearnt—that the sword makes history and the pen records it. The miserable string of battles and dates which was served out to us was a travesty of that most fascinating of subjects, the development of the peoples of the world. In that development, the prime factor has been thought. Against thought, the sword has been pathetically powerless. The material blade has no cutting edge against a spiritual force. It cannot make it, take it or break it. Like the seed that uproots the granite paving, the mustard seed of thought overthrows empires which are as passing as nationality is permanent. That is because men think nationally, not imperially. Thought is the mightiest power known to man. To-day where history is being made, thought is fermenting. Where it stagnates there is no history.

More important is that we are born into a universe of thought just as truly as we are all born citizens of some country. If we try to imagine ourselves living in the days of Julius Cæsar, what percentage of our ideas could we carry back with us to those days? Could we be said to be ourselves in any intelligible sense, if we thought as Cæsar and his people in their day?

We do not always realize that effective salvation must imply more than the salvation of the individual. It must mean the transformation of the thought that surrounds him. We may see something of the meaning of this by trying to imagine Jesus born in ancient Greece. Even if we imagined that He could have had the ideas He possessed, can we picture Him finding the ears to hear them and the lips to preach them?

The Christian evangel pre-supposes the Hebrew prophets and the atmosphere of thought which their work had created. Its continuance demands a mental as well as a moral atmosphere.

Here again we have another aspect of salvation, the redemption of thought. Suppose that a man were converted and sent to live amongst an entirely heathen population, and not allowed to speak to a soul about his new experience. How long would he be likely to retain it? Surely a mental background is needful for the effectiveness of conversion, and Christ's teaching filtering down through the thought of our age has provided this. One is not surprised that St. Paul's visit to Athens produced so small a result. Not that the Athenians who listened were profound philosophers; none the less the intellectual atmosphere of the country is breathed even by the unlearned, giving them not a knowledge of things such as the thinker possesses, but rather a certain tone and temper of mind. For example, can one imagine that the Buddhist teaching which has made so great an appeal to the ordinary man in Japan and China, could possibly flourish here, or be preached with acceptance in the streets? It is impossible, because Buddhism represents a mental outlook foreign to the thought of this land. When we speak of salvation, we do not always realize that salvation implies the redemption of thought, as well as of life, and not simply the individual's thought, but the habits of racial thought. Christ has not only provided salvation for men's souls, but for their minds, and has given to the man who is saved a chance of acquiring a mental outlook which will assist the development of the new life created in him. It is true that there are still many un-Christian habits of thought, though even so, few flourish openly. The collapse of the ideas of Nietzsche is a token of the impossibility of a radically un-Christian system becoming widespread. The general habit of the thought of the world to-day is influenced profoundly by Christ. It will be needful to dwell upon this for a moment for it is seldom fully realized.

Perhaps the clearest way of showing the transformation will be in setting out briefly, by way of comparison, the Christian idea of goodness along with the best type of pre-Christian ideal. The four cardinal virtues of Greece were wisdom, courage, self-control and justice. The Christian cardinal three are faith, hope and love. It seems strange that the two lists do not overlap in a single particular, yet the reason is not far to seek. The four Greek virtues have special relation to man and are exhibited in human relationships. The Christian three, as Aquinas said, have God as their object, bring men into true relationship with God, and are imparted by Him alone. They belong to the new relationship to God

which Jesus gave. Faith and hope spring
out of love. In the days when the
gods were regarded as capricious and
at times cruel, such trust in them could
not exist. Jesus taught that the nature
of God was love. This introduced a
new temper into life which is revealed
in the whole attitude of the civilized
world to life as a whole. When people
speak disparagingly of a veneer of
Christianity on Europe as the only result
of the impact of Christ's teaching for
2,000 years, they show little appreciation
of the difference of the modern and
the Greek attitude to life. Even those
who do not accept Christ's teaching
could never think of life purely in
terms of the Greek attitude to it. The
Greek and the Christian virtues alike
referred to the spirit in which a man
lived his life, but the spirit is not the
same. Faith and hope are based on
love to and of God; they represent
the assertion of the Christian spirit
against unbelief and pessimism, the twin

foes of religion. Modern man lives in a new world, made new not simply by the progress of science, but by the ideals of Jesus which have transformed all thought, and revalued all values. The man who does not think with Christ none the less is obliged to think differently because of Christ. Never could the Greek world-view recur to-day, however little may this fact be realized.

If it is necessary to make this clearer, consider the picture of the " high-minded man," upon whom Aristotle lavishes admiration. He tells us that " a high-minded man " is specially concerned with honours. Yet he will be only moderately pleased with great honours conferred on him feeling that they are not more, but perhaps less than his due. Since the people, however, have nothing better to offer him, he will accept them ; but such honour as is paid by ordinary folk on trivial grounds he will utterly despise as he deserves something better.

He equally despises dishonour, knowing it cannot be attached to such as he is. Little wonder Aristotle confesses that high-minded people seem to be supercilious. He says that since it is an inferiority to receive benefits, the "high-minded man" dislikes to do so and tries to return them with interest so as to make the original benefactor obliged to him, because he always aspires to superiority, and cannot bear to be told of benefits he has received, indeed he seems to forget them. He is not fond of praising people, but he will tell the truth except when he is ironical, although he will use irony in dealing with ordinary people.

To any Englishman, whether a professing Christian or not, such a man to-day would be regarded as contemptible, a prig, a "bounder." It is hard to realize that a great and good man like Aristotle could think such to be the ideal of manly character. If Aristotle could return to life, one imagines that a certain word in our tongue would puzzle him more than any other, the word gentleman. That the high-minded man could be gentle would pass Aristotle's understanding. The ideal of the gentle man testifies, as the world itself shows, to Galilee, not Greece. It is just one more indication of the way in which Jesus has turned the thought of the world upside down. He has given an entirely new idea of what is admirable in character. After all, the man who lives the Christ-life is revered by thousands who do not attempt to live it themselves. Jesus has once and for all saved us from such a false ideal of life and conduct as Aristotle's " high-minded " man exhibits.

We have only to look at the ideas which are the commonplace property of the ordinary man to-day, and to compare them with those of the ancient world, to realize how thoroughgoing is the transformation of the world's thought, brought about by Jesus. The watchword of the French revolution, a revolution avowedly anti-Christian, was Liberty, Equality, Fraternity. What chance would such an appeal have had in the ears of the ancient world ? Liberty, yes, at the discretion of the king or rulers, to small privileged classes. But when Plato eulogised freedom in Athens, half or more of the population were slaves, and to ask liberty for the slave would have appeared as ridiculous to him as an agitation to enfranchise dogs or horses would seem to us. Aristotle indeed expressly defended slavery as an example of natural law, whereby the more advanced subjugate to their own uses the inferior forms of life. If the unalienable right of every man to liberty is sung all over the civilized world to-day, the reason more than any other is that the principles of Jesus imply it.

Equality—what an empty word that seemed to any Greek, Roman or Jew ! Indeed it is meaningless in many ways still. All men are not born equal, either intellectually or morally, and there is only one sense in which one man is as good as another, in that all are the children of one heavenly Father. But no Greek ever thought the conception of Father Zeus implied that. The only meaning that may be attached to the claim for equality is the implication of the teaching of the Divine Fatherhood which Jesus gave.

Fraternity. Did any Jew ever think of the Gentile as a brother, or any Roman greet brother barbarian? To-day the term brother is common between all classes, not only in the Christian church but in such communities as the Masons and similar societies. Masonic lodges include men of different religions, but like the members of Kipling's mother lodge, they are all brethren. Who taught that but Jesus?

It has become our habit to see something of value in labour as labour, not merely in the product. A little

97

G

while ago I was looking at a sketch by a well-known artist, representing the cab of an express engine at night, with the figure of the driver silhouetted by the red glare of the open firebox door against the night sky, whilst the fireman, shovel in hand, fed the flames. It was a representation of skilled and responsible labour that dignifies the man whose task is to fulfil it. Yet what Greek would have chosen labour as a subject for art? Gods, heroes, warriors, beauty, all these inspired him, but not labour. The world has learnt the value of labour by looking at that workshop at Nazareth.

A little while ago, a collecting box was held out to me inscribed " Whatever your creed, you sympathize with suffering. Help the local hospital." I found myself wondering how such an appeal would have sounded in the ancient world. To the strong, the weakness of the weak seemed contemptible. Cassius derides Cæsar to Brutus, because when he was in Spain, he had a fever, and shook, crying with pale lips for drink. Why should a man of such a feeble temperament rule the world, he demanded. To-day no one would think with Cassius that such an appeal was a sign of weakness of character. A new sympathy has come into the world's outlook on pain, because of One who went about healing the sick. " Whatever your creed " said the legend. One wonders. The Quran says that " Whatever ye suffer is your own fault." Buddhism says suffering is the karma of a previous existence being worked out inexorably. The tenderness of the world to-day to suffering is the result of the transforming work of Jesus who has turned the world's thought upside down. It is said that in the East, one may still trace the old caravan routes by the flowers. The caravan halted for the night, and the beasts were foddered. The seeds that were in the fodder scattered, and so it

is that on the hill passes are still to be
found patches of colour, flowers that
belonged originally to the plains.
In such a way, one may trace the path
of the influence of Jesus in the transformed thought that has everywhere
followed the preaching of His name.
The average man little realizes how
thoroughly his habits of thought are
shot through and through with sentiments that owe their existence to
the new thought Jesus gave to man.
Heine, in an eloquent passage, describes
the gods banqueting on Olympus. In
the midst of the merriment, a pale Jew,
staggering under the load of his
cross enters, throws the cross on the
table, and the gods vanish like smoke
before wind. The Jew and his
cross confront the world alone. But
it was not merely that the gods vanished,
their mental level went also, and the
strata of thought that produced them.
To-day the world thinks as it was
taught to think from Galilee. Michelet

once said that Galilee was all very well, but he was thirsty and could quench that thirst only in the deep springs of the inspiration of Hellas. If Michelet had to drink all that those springs contained, one thinks he would find the draught rather bitter.

The transformation of thought is a necessity to the effectiveness of salvation. The mission field witnesses this. In the early days of missions, good men with an enthusiasm one cannot but admire and at a risk one can hardly exaggerate, went out to preach Christ, the Christ that the Western world knew, in Western ways, and taught the characteristic theology of their days. That they succeeded at all is surely due to the attractive power of the gospel which was not destroyed by all those handicaps. But the few converts they made were necessarily westernized, the camp followers of the missionary. Unwittingly the mistake was repeated against which St. Paul stood out so nobly. He objected to the Gentile convert being Judaized in order to be Christianized. Yet these were westernized in order to be Christianized ; a short range policy in every way. None other was possible perhaps, but we are realizing to-day that educational work rather than evangelism is the key. The hope of sowing and reaping without ploughing is vain. A mental outlook has to be created, and the thought of the peoples concerned, won, before they can have what ultimately they must have—a Christianity of their own. Yet there are some who still doubt the need of educational missions !

We talk about apostolic Christianity as if it were the final form and ideal of all Christianity, and one from which we have lapsed in many ways. Rather should we think of it as an early type, pure and simple in its own way, may be, but one that has been developed greatly to fit our own needs. If some of those who so admire apostolic Christianity could be placed by a time machine in apostolic days, they might experience a very considerable shock, in finding that their ideal was hardly recognizable. The reason is that the mental background is wholly changed, and the man whose outlook has been shaped by modern science would find it hard to acclimatize himself to a world that thought in terms of animism, to whose thought disease was devil possession, and to which magic lay on the borderline of religion.

No life can be lived in isolation from the mental environment of the day, and to save men and then leave them in an atmosphere where the breath of God never stirred, if indeed that were possible, would be to waste their salvation. All will admit that, but not all will draw the necessary corollary that the salvation of a nation's thought is the pre-condition of its being Christianized. We of the West have still to learn this fully. We westernize our converts far too much. For example, the belief of the East in re-incarnation is foreign to our thought and we accordingly assume there is something un-Christian or anti-religious in it, and teach our converts to abandon it. Why? Plato held such views without any impiety or detriment to his character, and if these views raise philosophical difficulties, they also explain some things, and have distinctly a moral significance. One cannot see why we should not allow the East to work out its own conception of Christianity even to the mingling with it of certain of its own characteristic strains of thought. Our Western philosophy of life is not the only one that can accompany Christianity, and if Christ is to save the East, the East must find Him for itself through its own teachers and thinkers. We can do no more than start the work. But if those thinkers and teachers cast off the age-long habits of thought that are the heritage of the East and westernize their presentation of Christianity, it will fail in their hands. Their task is to find the link between their ways of thought and the Christian evangel. The Eastern conception of Christ is not likely to be the same as our own, but why should that be a hindrance to the understanding of One whose star was seen in the East? The Eastern form of Christianity will be touched with Buddhist, Hindu, Islamic, Parsi and other ideas, just as ours is touched by Hebrew, Roman and Greek thought. It will be different from ours, but when the East has learnt to think its own thoughts in terms of Christ, the evangelization of the world will be at hand.

The case of Africa, however, is different, for she has no great indigenous civilization, but only ways of thought that in any case must sooner or later be outgrown, as indeed they have been outgrown by other nations. Africa will probably modify the conceptions she has received from the West, but not greatly. India must find her own Christ, and so must China. The salvation of India means that the characteristic ways of Indian thought must be baptised with the spirit of Jesus and transformed. Yet even after they have been transformed they will be Indian, not Western.

One sometimes hears the crude objection against missionary effort, that each nation's religion is well fitted to its needs, and that it is an impertinence on our part to interfere. It is noteworthy that those who say this seldom make the same application to methods of government, to which it should apply much more closely, one would imagine. But the truth that makes such a statement in any way plausible is that each nation has its own ethos, and the presentation of an Anglicized form of Christianity seldom meets this. That is why salvation must imply a mental as well as a moral aspect.

To take a long range view of things, it seems likely that the next few centuries will be marked by the percolation throughout the world of the Christian attitude to life and the transvaluation of values in the light of it. But the old type of Christianization will not continue. We can evangelize uneducated peoples, and in so doing make them imitate us. But now we have elected to educate, we must be prepared for those we have educated departing from our standards of Christianity. That will not mean departing from Christ. No nation that has ever had a pure form of Christianity has given it up for any other faith. But we shall see a new and composite conception of Christianity growing up, to which all nations will contribute. The ideal of the kingdom of God is one in which all nations can join. " They shall bring the glory and honour of the nations into it." The kingdom will embrace all the characteristic ways of thinking, but with an emphasis amongst them chosen by Christ's way. It may be that we shall be rewarded for anything we have contributed towards the evangelization of the world by receiving back from other races their own conception of Christ, thus finding visions we had failed entirely to see.

Christ, who saved the thought of the ancient world, re-fashioning it after His own, will do the same in the nations where His name is now being preached. Until that process is complete, His work is incomplete. A Christian nation implies a Christian thinking nation, perhaps it need imply no more. The evangelization of the mind is just as important as the saving of the soul. Indeed it is difficult to see what the latter can mean apart from the former, and what is true of the individual is also true here of the mass. The salvation of the world means that the world must learn to think Christlikely and only when the thought of the world has been brought into captivity in obedience to Christ, shall we have a truly Christian world—never otherwise.

From the Standpoint
of Psychology

V

THE TRANSFORMATION
OF COMMERCE

THE TRANSFORMATION OF COMMERCE

THE change between the outlook of the Middle Ages and that of the present day is in no point more marked than in the attitude taken towards the future of the world and its peoples. To monks, who had fled its perils, the world seemed in evil case. There was no hope for a future on earth. Classical writers familiarized the Early Church with the idea of a world proceeding in cycles of decay and reconstruction, and this took Christian shape in the notion that the world was destined to perish at the Second Advent, and then be set up once more in heaven. In the year 1,000, churches were crowded with fearsome worshippers who believed that the end of all things was at hand. The critical year passed, but not the expectation of the end. The world was evil, and the long-suffering

H

of God alone allowed time for repentance
ere the final judgment was staged. Under
these circumstances, it is not surprising
that salvation meant an individual
pardon at the Last Judgment, rather
than any reconstitution of human
society on earth.

The revival of learning, the Refor-
mation, and the growing power of
the people, in many lands at least, all
contributed to a change in outlook
which slowly came to pass. But it
was not until the idea of evolution,
misread as necessary progress, entered
into the mind of the age, that belief
in progress became well-nigh universal.
The idea has far more superstructure
than basis, and may therefore collapse
any time the temper of the age changes,
but it is being reinforced not by
biological or sociological considerations
so much as by the sense of spiritual
values. There seems no reason to
assume that these are so slight that
they will be wiped away by any sudden

destruction of the conditions under which they are being fashioned. The speculations of science as to the ultimate fate of the universe by expansion or radiation are far too remote in the period assigned for their operation, and it may be said, too hazardous to form a serious obstacle to the belief that there is for mankind a destiny on earth that has hardly yet begun to develop. If man may be on earth for a million million years, as Sir James Jeans has suggested, the possibilities of social evolution are boundless, and the ultimate fate of this planet far too remote to make us specially concerned with the differences between those who say the universe is running down and those who say it may be wound up again. To all intents and purposes, man has a span long enough to call a practical eternity before him, " barring cosmic accidents."

It is true that evolution may mean retrogression as well as progress, but

since the first Christian era, despite
temporary setbacks, the trend of spiritual
evolution has been definitely upward,
and the present age displays social
conditions which, however defective,
are nearer the ideals of the New
Testament than those of any previous
age. Such facts encourage us to believe
in a future for mankind in which
the teaching of Jesus will actually be
applied to the life of the world. That
will mean social salvation. The salvation brought by Christ means more
than the resetting of individual lives
towards God. It means the renovation
of society, a social order based on
the principles of the Sermon on the
Mount.

That individual lives should be lived
on those principles is preached from
every pulpit. That war should be
abolished as inconsistent with them is
a conviction that has gathered great
strength during the years of the
aftermath of the European War. But

it is strange how little yet is said of what is the most essential of all things, if there is to be a Christian social order, namely the Christianization of commerce. It may be that we are as yet unready even to envisage the enormousness of the change this will produce, but it remains that the salvation of society is impossible under the present system, and if we had the faith and courage of the early church in setting itself against the evil of slavery and Cæsarism in the social order, we should be less afraid of our task.

The impact of Christianity on commerce means to many earnest minded people the mitigation of some of the evils of the present system by personal benevolence and consideration, the care of employees, pensions for old servants, and some limitation perhaps of personal profit. All this, whilst certainly a gain, leaves the root of the matter untouched. The tap-root of evil in the commercial system is the fact that the common

denominator of business life is personal
gain, irrespective of social gain. True,
business is necessary to social life, but
that is not the reason for its existence.
A new business is started for the profit
of those engaged in it, and apart from
that cannot continue.

The evils of this system, where the
social utility, the moral worth, the value
to the future of the business in question
are all subordinate to the sole issue
of profit, has caused many to demand
the abolition of the whole capitalistic
society. Yet the abolition of capitalism
cannot be said, even by the most enthusiastic supporter of that doctrine, to
be an end in itself. To what end then
will it lead? Constituted as we are,
there is no indication that if a man
has no personal interest in his work
beyond the necessity of earning enough
to live, there will be any work really
well done. The personal element is
ineradicable. Even in the most self
sacrificing form of altruism, mother-love,

the personal element is marked, as is shown by the fact that the harsh stepmother is as familiar in fact and fiction as the devoted mother. The idea that any race of men can be so imbued with the love of society that they will work as society directs, without personal choice or initiative, argues little knowledge of the fundamental psychological mechanisms, but it still remains that the personal element, so utterly necessary, need not be that of pure monetary gain. Indeed, some of the greatest "capitalists" have little use for money personally. It is the power and responsibility that money brings which attracts them. It is likely that in the long range view, capitalism as we now know it, will go, but Socialism may bring its own evils which will neutralise any benefits from the change. The ethics of Christianity do not necessarily imply any particular system of production and exchange, even though some systems are certainly easier to fit into the Christian scheme of things than others. What it does imply is a change of attitude as regards the aim of the world's work.

The worst condemnation of the present system is not that thereby money is unequally distributed and that many can gather where they have not strawed. It is that a man could discover something of great gain to the community at large, and use the discovery purely for personal profit. As it is, a man might conceivably discover a cure for cancer, and instead of publishing it, take a few rich patients at a great fee and become a millionaire whilst others died for lack of the knowledge. He would be legally within his rights, because the right to amass personal gain by commerce with the community is a primary one, in the present state of things. A man can be punished for depriving the community of what is its own, but he cannot be touched if he who owes all to the society which bred and fed him, uses what he has, to extort from it excessive personal gain. It may be said that the case suggested is extreme and improbable. Let us hope it is, but that does not alter the fact that it would be legally possible. Still, a milder example may serve. By means of the " Trust " or big combine, an artificial price can be put on articles of common use or consumption so that, as in actual well-known cases, the directors of the combine have amassed millions, because the public are in their hands and must pay any price they ask for the goods which are necessary. Once again, wealth and the power and privileges it bestows depend not on worth or service, but on an organisation artificially to inflate prices. The State has failed to control the Trusts, and the Trusts bid fair to control the State.

Let us see where our argument has led us. The present system stands condemned, not because it is capitalism, but because it allows the motive of business to be personal gain merely, and because such gain is often irrespective of service rendered. It also allows power in the community to be handed over to those who have shown more rapacity than capacity, to account for their possessing it. On the other hand, the personal element cannot be taken from work without irreparable loss. Nevertheless, Christianity cannot be committed to any particular system, because it is not the system but the spirit that makes the moral worth of a man's work.

The salvation of commerce, therefore, means the bringing in of a new spirit, and this spirit must find its own methods. Christianity cannot commit itself to the support of any one method. It must preach as it has never yet preached, however, that our fundamental duty as individuals is to serve the community, and that in no other way can we even realise our own individuality. So little do we understand this, that we still think it our first task to secure our own position, and then by way of charity to give somewhat of our time or money to " social service," which generally means acting as an ambulance to pick up the casualties of the system under which we have prospered.

Under a Christian system, social service would include the ordinary occupations of daily life, though there would be a necessary elimination of gambling and similar forms of exchange where no gain to the community results. Every man would think in terms of the motto : Service before Self. Realizing that humanity is one family, to serve the family would be the primary duty, and work would be valued according as it was of worth to society. Now it is thought by many that a man who is wealthy enough to do nothing but amuse himself is to be envied. Indeed, he is sometimes praised as giving employment to others, and needing none himself. Under a rational, let alone a Christian order, such a man would be regarded as a social defaulter and treated accordingly.

Some professions have already shown the way towards this ideal. The clerical and medical professions are trained to put service before self, and any clergyman or medical man who was known to use his profession as a means merely of amassing wealth, would be rightly ostracised by all his fellow members. The same is true of some civil services. In all cases the members of these professions live under the same conditions as the rest of the community. They are not, like Plato's guardians, kept from the use of money. But to them it is an understood thing that money is to be subordinate to service. No medical man, for example, is allowed to profit by any discovery he may make in medicine and surgery. He must publish his results for common use. Yet there is scope in all these professions for personal interest and ambition, so that the objection that unless financial gain is possible, work will suffer, is rebutted.

It is clear, therefore, that the transformation of commerce on these lines does not present an impracticable task, however difficult it may be. The Christianization or salvation of commerce lies in adapting life to the Sermon on the Mount. The question remains how far are we to take that teaching as an ideal capable of realisation in this present world. The answer to that question demands that we avoid certain common errors that have clouded the understanding of the Christ's teaching. The first is that He gave a system of doctrine. His teaching may be made such by addition and subtraction, by multiplying precepts and dividing truth. But the saying of the Fourth Gospel that if any man would do the will he should know of the teaching expresses exactly what that teaching is—practical directions for doing God's will, and that is far from being the same thing as a system of doctrine.

The same saying explains another mistake, that Christ's teaching is meant for all men. It is not. It is meant for those who will to do the will of God. To the rest it is folly, or at best a pretty and impossible ideal. The Beatitudes are the eight steps that lead to Calvary, and the man who has no intention of following on that sacred path, finds them as the Jew found the Cross, a stumbling block ; or, as the Greek saw it, foolishness. The teaching becomes clear as one does the will, never otherwise.

A third error is the belief that the teaching of Jesus was meant to be taken literally. He who gave the Spirit was no giver of the letter of the law. He knew that direct precepts can never be for all time. The beloved " Torah " of the Jew has been forced to bow to the necessities of time and circumstance. No one, to-day, can live exactly according to the law of Moses. A strict Muhammadan could not live in the polar regions, for the fasting month might fall when there is no night, and the command to fast in the day would result in starvation, as indeed was actually the case in one instance. Some of Wesley's rules are more honoured in the breach than in the observance. But the teaching of Jesus remains intact, because He gave principles not precepts. Paul gave both. Many Pauline precepts have lost their force, but nothing Jesus said was ever abrogated by time. To realise the greatness of Jesus, one had but to compare him with St. Paul, who was perhaps the greatest man who ever lived, both in his thought and his influence. Yet, beside Jesus, Paul is a pigmy.

Those who argue that the Sermon on the Mount is impractical because we are told therein to " Give to him that asketh thee," have not read far enough. Otherwise they would have read " Give not that which is holy unto the dogs." How can we both give and not give ? This contrast alone shows that these sayings were not meant to be interpreted in a strict literality, but we do them scant justice if we call them Eastern hyperbole. The point is surely that the Sermon on the Mount contrasts the spirit of the world with the spirit of Christ. Give to everyone. Why, what are they to me, says the man of the world ? Every man has a claim on you, says Jesus, and to him you must render what you can. " Silver and gold have I none, but such as I have I give thee." That is the spirit. It is easy to ridicule the saying of turning the other cheek, but is it not the very word of victory ? The world says " Hit back." Jesus says, " Suffer and hold on. Let him strike and strike again. Hold on." Is that not the way of victory ? Has the " hit back " policy ever done more than breed war ? If there is to be world peace, it will be only by the practice of non-resistance. It has taken 2,000 years to see this, but the policy of the Sermon on the Mount is, as is becoming abundantly clear to-day, the only way to the abolition of war. The teaching of the Sermon on the Mount is not only practical. It is the teaching that must be followed if the world is not to commit suicide.

The salvation of society, then, means the putting into practice of the Sermon on the Mount. We have emphasized the fact that commerce must be the point of attack by the Christian strategist, for should once we have a Christian commercial system, the conversion of the world would be well nigh accomplished. The enormous difficulties of Christianizing commerce need not be repeated. Yet no Christian can doubt it should be done, and on the long range view what should be has always been more powerful than what is. It would be an insult to the might of God to

I

think that what should be could not be. If we would preach the salvation of commerce as insistently as we preach individual salvation, we should have taken the first step, which is to make men believe in its possibility. This done, the rest would in its own, which means in God's time, follow. But until we have attacked the problem of transforming the ideals of business, the possibility of a Christian social order vanishes. Jesus's teaching would be the salvation of the world's trade, not only in the spiritual sense, but in the literal. Nationalism, tariff walls, mistrust of the foreigner in every nation mean logically that each be left to trade with itself, and the evils of the present are the result of that policy. A Christian ideal would expand the world's trade to an extent undreamed of in the widest aims of mankind.

*From the Standpoint
of Psychology*

VI

IS SALVATION FOR ALL?

IN raising this question, we are not turning back to the dry bones of the Calvinist and Arminian controversy. Quite another issue is before us. There are a large number of earnest Christians who have experienced what they call "conversion." They are sure they are "saved." There are others who, without any crisis, or as it has been called by Prof. De Sanctis, "fulminant" conversion, none the less are conscious of the power and presence of Christ in their lives. To them He represents the greatest of realities. Yet these do not exhaust by any means the number of those who cannot be denied the name of Christian. There are tens of thousands of men and women who have no sense of any personal relationship to Christ. They go, sometimes regularly, more often occasionally, to a place of worship, and have an admiration and reverence for His character. They would not speak evil of Him, nor would they allow themselves to commit any flagrant violation of the principles of His teaching. But beyond that they are just the creatures of this age and world, accepting the usual habits and outlook of their times and neighbours, and if one were to ask them if they were " saved " they would escape the question, or the questioner, with the usual embarrassed reticence of the average Englishman.

Are we to count people of this type amongst the "saved"? Do they wish to be so reckoned? On the other hand, are we to call them unsaved? An understandable common charity makes us speak of them when they die as amongst the redeemed, and our own sense of the love of God will not allow us to exclude such people from His Fatherly mercies. Yet again the question raises itself; if these are saved, why is a very different state called salvation in other cases ? Considerations of this sort enforce the question " Is Salvation for All ? " If we answer Yes, then we must either admit that salvation has very varied manifestations, or else try to show that extremely different experiences are at root the same thing. The former seems the only likely method. If the ecstatic rapture, the fervent conviction of those who have a conscious experience of a religious renewal, have nothing to do with their salvation, and such salvation belongs equally to them and to the average man who has no such experience at all, these experiences are inconsequential. This is the last thing those who experience them will admit, and moreover, is an unlikely thesis to put forth in any case. If then salvation is a term with wide meaning, what types of salvation are possible ? The answer is that the meaning of salvation will be found to depend on the religious experience concerned, and an analysis of certain main types of experience will prove the best way of facing the question.

Psychologists have frequently recognised a distinction between the " active " and " passive " types of religious experience, and in the main, this distinction is a good one, though nobody is purely of either type. We will, however, make a division which for convenience sake, may be called the Jacob and Esau types.

Esau represents more closely than any other Biblical character the average Anglo-Saxon male, a type perennial, and one which is found in thousands and tens of thousands amongst public schoolboys. He has the virtues of the sportsman. He is impulsive, generous, quick to anger, and yet ready to drop the quarrel, neither vindictive or mean. He is kindly, hospitable, a lover of animals, a good father and husband, and by no means an irreligious or godless man. He has no objection to church, though the golf course is more attractive on a Sunday morning, but if he were asked to speak of his conversion he would disclaim any such thing at once. In short, is the ordinary decent Englishman " saved," and if so, in what sense ?

Jacob, on the other hand, began his career as a scoundrel. His idea of brotherliness was to filch a birthright for a mess of pottage, he meanly deceived his old father, and bolstered up the lie he told him by reference to the name of God. He cheated Laban, and his idea of religion was a bargain at Bethel, in which he offered God ten per cent. commission on any favours He might bestow on him. There is no sign of repentance till he comes into touch with Esau, and then his repentance was sheer funk. By the side of this person, Esau is a hero, and his forgiveness magnificent. Yet, though Jacob's type generally repents through fear, the experience at Peniel was catastrophic. In one of the most

vivid narratives of the Old Testament
we read of the anxious man, pacing
the ground in the darkness, unable to
sleep, terrified lest the well deserved
vengeance of Esau fall on him. Suddenly
he is gripped. For a moment he thinks
it is Esau's grip, and one can imagine
the guilty man screaming with terror.
As he struggles in the grip of his
own conscience, a new experience
comes to him. The vivid story of
the wrestling is too grand to be made
an argument with any fundamentalist
whose Western imagination with pedestrian literality insists that some angelic
being wrestled with Jacob. Let him
think as he will. A great spiritual
struggle went on in Jacob's soul, whoever
or whatever his adversary.

Jacob was beaten, and the very fact
he had to yield his name without knowing
that of his foe, was a sign, for the name
was the last thing an Oriental would
have revealed to an adversary. To
know the name was to have power

over its owner. His thigh was out
of joint. He was helpless, and at that
very moment he won through. He
had learnt his lesson. His weakness
was the secret of strength. Hitherto
he had prevailed by cunning. Now he
wins by renunciation. A spiritual crisis
had taken place, and a new man with a
new name passed over Peniel with the
sunlight on his tired, triumphant face.

From that day onward Jacob was a
new man. The name is but a sign of a
change that went deep. The old scheming,
crafty Jacob was reborn as Israel, a
converted man. The story of Peniel
has had its analogies in many lives.
It is undoubted that there are men
who are capable of villainy, and yet
once turned, will reveal a truly spiritual
nature. On the other hand Esau is
probably as incapable of villainy as of
such a spiritual crisis and subsequent
experience. Is the Esau type " saved " ?

The historic Esau could claim the
words of Jesus as fitting his own case.

Those who forgive men their trespasses He said, will be forgiven of God; Esau's forgiveness of Jacob puts him within this promise. This suggests that the theology of Jesus was wider than that of orthodox Christianity. Salvation, He declared, came to the house of Zacchæus when he promised to restore what he had exacted, and give of his gains to the poor. Orthodoxy insists on repentance and faith, and after all, this was what Zacchæus manifested. He showed his repentance by his effort to put right the wrongs he had done, and his faith by accepting this as the right way. In many a case, men of the Esau type have done the same thing. They have made amends and set themselves to try to do the right thing in life, and it may well be that this is their salvation. Because it is unconnected with any definite religious experience, we are apt to disregard its significance. But we cannot believe that the Jesus of history, Whose catho-

licity would not allow Him to forbid
the man who without following Him
did His works, will reject the man
who does the right, just because he
is lacking in religious outlook. It is
the question of the Numinous and the
moral once more. Esau's type have
not much sense of the Numinous, but
they have the moral sense, and their
salvation lies not in their works, but
in their faith in the right which the
works reveal.

That any doubt should exist regarding
this, indicates how the original conception
of salvation has been narrowed. Zacchæus
received salvation from Jesus, knowing
nothing of an atoning death. His salvation came through his acceptance of
Jesus into his home and his promise
to " go straight." The dying thief
had no thought that the Fellow Sufferer
was dying for his sins, but made a simple
personal response to the silent appeal
of Christ's purity. The Philippian gaoler
was bidden, without any particular

qualification, to believe in the Lord Jesus Christ. All these men were saved, and to limit salvation either to evangelical or to sacramental experience is a proceeding that cannot be reconciled with the New Testament.

The salvation of the Esau type will not be on the same lines as that of Jacob. Jacob, we admitted, was capable of much more evil, and at the same time, of greater spirituality than Esau. All very highly spiritual natures have corresponding capacities for more than ordinary human evil. We, who see only their outward lives, may have thought their habit of denouncing themselves as the chief of sinners a pious exaggeration. If we knew their hearts we should realise that they speak sincerely. They know from how much they have been and are being saved. Esau has no sense of having committed any great sin. He never does what " isn't done." Hence, poor Esau, bidden to repent in sackcloth and ashes, cannot quite

see why he should. His conscience
is not complacent, but, at the same
time, it is not condemnatory. Frankly,
he thinks he might be better, and yet
he knows he might well be worse.

Ought we to expect from Esau what
we expect from Jacob? Evangelical
Christianity has seldom been capable
of accommodating him, because it has
not understood him. It has appealed
to him to be a Jacob. It has preached
to him Jacob's type of conversion.
He does not understand, for he is not
and cannot be, Jacob. The Roman
Church has accommodated him, perhaps
a trifle too readily. Its strength has
been in its recognition of this type
of human character, its weakness in
compromising with, rather than com-
prehending it. Rome has reduced its
claim to a few definite commands and
certain specific discipline, which Esau
has accepted, as he accepts the rules
of his club. He knows he has a soul,
though it is somewhat of a mystery

to him, but he reflects that the church, like the doctor, should know what is right, and submits accordingly.

Evangelical Christianity has been led by men with a burning spiritual experience but insufficient appreciation of psychological types to realize that what is for them is not in the same way for all. They well understand the sinner who can be converted to sainthood, not so well the average man of the Esau pattern. They offer to him things of which he is not really capable. Jesus spoke of ground that was capable of thirty, sixty and an hundredfold increase. Evangelical preaching has been too apt to expect the hundredfold from the thirtyfold. It is perfectly true to say that Christianity recognizes no inner grades and esoteric teaching, that its message is for all alike, and yet Jesus was definite in saying that those who had ears to hear heard what others did not, that according to man's faith so was it to him. He certainly recognized the existence of a class from which less was to be expected, because they had been thought capable of using but one or two talents, where others had five. He led us to expect that a return proportionate, not equal, would be required in the day of reckoning. Jesus knew far too much about the complexities of human nature, and varieties of religious experience, to treat all men alike, or expect from all a similar response. But has His church always shown such discrimination? Has it not far too often insisted that there is one way of entering the narrow gate, one way of accepting the gift of the Kingdom? It has left aside those who cannot find that way in the hope that somehow they will change their nature and find it, or that God will work some miracle and find it for them.

The realisation that many do not respond to the evangelical appeal has had the effect, in some cases, of making

145

K

evangelists anxious at all costs to open the way to converts. Some of them give the impression that the Master is delighted to receive on any terms, anyone who will simply sign a card, hold up a hand, or express a momentary desire to be saved. That certainly was not characteristic of the Jesus of the Gospels. He rejected, in a summary way, several volunteers who were not of the type He wanted. Such, He declared, were not fit, " no good " for the Kingdom. He had no place for the waverer, the man who had not counted the cost. An easy universalism was never preached by Jesus. He required a decision that must be ratified in life. Some evangelical methods undoubtedly have placed the emphasis on the decision, as if it were an end in itself, in flat contradiction to the method of Jesus.

On the other hand, there has often been neglect of the class who, if one might so put it, make no decision, and yet show more ratification than many who do make a decision. The evangelical experience of salvation will never be theirs, but, directly or indirectly, their lives have testified to the spirit of Jesus in them. To this class may well have belonged some of those publicans and sinners who heard Jesus speak, but of whom there is no record in the Gospels. They may not have become known among the " brethren," they may have continued amongst their own class doing their usual work, but none the less may have entered into life, because in their own way, and under the conditions laid down for them by temperament, circumstance, and other factors, they responded to the appeal to the Godward side of their nature. Is the type of salvation, cultivated in the evangelical churches, the only type? Compare it with the kind of appeal Jesus Himself made, with the results He Himself saw, and one will hesitate to answer Yes. " Many are called but few chosen," He said. We are all too apt to declare "All are called and all chosen." Moreover, those who were most sure they were chosen, He said, were rejected, and those who were last, He said would be first.

Have we realised sufficiently the significance of the habit of Jesus in consorting with publicans and sinners? Removed from our gaze by the passing of 2,000 years, these friends of His have become very different in our view from what they were. Now they are almost saints, not sinners. Yet, to their own day, they would represent a crowd as coarse as one can meet on a race course or in a slum public house. If any Christian to-day mixed socially with these people, we might find ourselves not a little astonished, and we should certainly call him "eccentric." So Jesus horrified the respectable classes of His day. Had He gone as John went, to rebuke them, that would have been an altogether different thing. But He mingled with them and dined with them, and "they all murmured" in scandalised tones, which would certainly be heard again to-day under similar circumstances. Even good folk, who admired Him, were perplexed that He could find any pleasure in such companionship. We are not told that He condemned them. He spoke to them of the Kingdom of God.

Is it possible that His motive was to make a protest against the prevailing opinion which excluded these men from the synagogue, because they were guilty of certain disreputable types of wrongdoing, yet allowed other types of sinners to be unchallenged? If so, may He not still be protestant against our similar classifications? If a man won a big lottery prize, many churches would call on him to resign his membership, yet amongst that membership a man whose business methods are those of pure speculation goes unchallenged. If a churchwarden is heard to use unparliamentary language, at once his fitness for office is questioned, but if he speaks bitterly and uncharitably, it is not thought worse than bad taste. If a deacon were in the habit of having an evening pint of beer at a public house his position would be at the least precarious. But if he were a sweater in business, would his position be as insecure ?

One cannot resist the inference that our standards of wrong-doing are often artificial. A certain class of sin excludes a man from religious fellowship, whilst another class, less coarse perhaps but worse morally, is overlooked. During the war I met in hospital scores of men who assured me they were not religious. They drank whenever they got the chance, swore continually, though they made valiant attempts to check the habit when the Padre was amongst them, and whenever they had a shilling, endowed the bookmakers. For these reasons they knew they were outsiders, and save for parade services, never saw the inner side of a church door. Yet they were brave, kindly, patient, thoughtful of others, wonderfully tender to their sick comrades. Why should such fine material be cast aside just because of habits which, however foolish and thoughtless, are not in any sense mortal sin? Once more we are amongst the Esau type, with its characteristic virtues and its incapacity for much spiritual vision. But is not salvation for Esau? "Hast thou but one blessing, my father? Bless me, even me also, O my father."

A little while ago, I was asked to join in a group discussion upon the question: "Is the evangelical experience for all?" As a psychologist, I cannot say it is, though speaking theologically, one thinks it ought to be. The universality of God's blessings is not now questioned. When the old Calvinist-Arminian controversy died away, it was because the extreme Calvinists had not sufficient forces to hold their position. The Arminians were left in possession of the field, and the opinion passed into the general thought of the day that all are alike capable of experiencing the grace that is offered them. In the same way, we assume that a capacity for enjoying artistic or musical pleasure is common to the whole race, yet it is notoriously true that certain individuals show no capacity whatever in those directions. Since this is a minor matter, we do not concern ourselves with it, beyond declaring that it is their loss.

Yet, is not the parallel with religious experience close, and must we not be prepared to find that many are extremely unlikely to share the evangelical experience ? That surely cannot imply that they are lost souls, but merely that their type is that which lives in the world of the senses, with limited spiritual capacities. This is their nature, not their sin, and such children of the Father cannot be excluded from His love and mercy because they were not born to see what others see.

The Esau type, whilst not sharing the keen spiritual experiences of the Jacob type, can none the less find their escape from self through Christ. It is not, we repeat, their moral code that marks out how far they are saved. It is their sense of something more than the self-centred, or, as Eucken called it, the petty life, which has given to them that loyalty which lifts a man from self to something higher than self, and led them to that service which is the life of the redeemed. They may never know what they owe to Christ, yet to Him, and to Him alone, do they owe it. They are His not because of their direct acknowledgment of Him, but because the life they have found is the life He gives.

Is salvation for all? Yes. Is the evangelical experience for all? Not of necessity consciously. The unsaved, if such there be, are those who have not found the way that leads out of self to service. Of all human qualities, as Josiah Royce and Bernard Bosanquet have insisted, loyalty is pre-eminently the religious quality. No man who has followed the leading of the spirit of God so as to find some escape from self can be entirely unsaved. The title of Jesus to the name Saviour does not rest in the Bible alone. It lies in the fact that He above all has led men to find the way of salvation, and by His life and death has proved Himself the Captain and Author of salvation to the millions who have come under His influence. As that influence widens, He will be to millions more what He has been to these, for there is no other way, no other name, that can compare with His. The Prince of Peace rides on His white horse " conquering and to conquer."

*From the Standpoint
of Psychology*

VII

FOR WHOM CHRIST DIED
IN VAIN

FOR WHOM CHRIST DIED
IN VAIN

SALVATION, we have said, is for all. Yet all are not saved. Who are the saved and who the unsaved is not for man to judge. It is the prerogative of God. Yet we cannot speak of salvation without the thought of the unsaved, and there is one story which, above all others, shows who was the man who went unsaved in the very presence of salvation, Judas Iscariot.

It is a story that seems incredible. That a disciple who, probably for three years, had been in the company of Christ, could go straightway from His presence to betray Him, passes our comprehension. No miracle is harder to understand than this miracle of sin. He saved others, Judas He could not save—so might His enemies have taunted Him. But why?

A question like this cannot be evaded. Yet, to blame Judas does not answer it, and we shall not try to blame or defend him. Our task is to attempt a psychological reconstruction of his motives rather than to moralize on them, and if our reconstruction must be provisional only, the main outline would probably command the consent of most psychologists.

Apparently, the man who set down the Holy Grail, and went out into the night to betray, began with a very different spirit. That he was admitted to the Twelve guarantees his previous character and his sincerity at first. The insight of Jesus told Him who would be the traitor, but the others did not know, and Judas himself probably did not. An act such as his is often as much a surprise to its perpetrator as to others. The fact that he was chosen as treasurer of the little company shows he was trusted and unsuspected to the end.

The first hint comes from the name Iscariot—man of Kerioth. He was the Southerner of the group. The rest were Northerners. A certain antagonism between north and south is not unusual. Witness the civil war of America, the highlander and lowlander in Scotland, whilst, even with ourselves, the north regards the south as a slenderer and less virile race, whilst the south retorts against the north country uncouthness.

The New Testament witnesses to the contempt of the south for the Galilean with his betraying accent. His was the land from which no prophet came. Judas was likely to come to the band of disciples with such a prejudice in his mind. Naturally the rest had something in common which he did not share. In this he may have felt himself aggrieved. Many have come to a group amongst whom they have to live and work, offer no special ground for notice, are even reserved and apparently unwishful of being noticed, and then throw the blame on those who have, so they declare, offered them no welcome. Judas may well have thought that the fellowship should adapt itself to him rather than he to it. Such an attitude illustrates a common cause of those minor social tragedies that often lead to major results. The instincts of self-preservation are behind our shyness in face of strangers, and like all instinctive activities are liable to aberration.

It is the old story of the superiority and inferiority sense becoming the cause of a complex. The mechanic who despises the labourer is almost sure to be acutely sensitive to the idea that the " black-coat " despises him. Superiority and inferiority senses are the Scylla and Charybdis of the mind stream.

Judas probably felt his superiority first. His aloofness caused him some loneliness which he attributed to the " clannishness " of the Galileans who did not want him. Possibly the office he held was an attempt on their part, or, more probably, on the part of Jesus, to bring him into closer fellowship and assure him that he was valued amongst them. Judas preferred to nurse a grievance. A grievance is an excuse for self-sympathy. That is its attraction to many minds. But sympathy is a social sentiment, belonging to the group sense, and to reverse the stream, turning inwards what should flow outwards, is never healthy mentally.

This loss of the sense of fellowship may account for the story of Judas's dishonesty, an unpardonable meanness against the trust of the band of poor men who allowed him to administer the sacrifices they made for those poorer still. It is not wholly fanciful to imagine that he may have excused himself on the ground that he, of superior birth, could not endure the hardships of following a Master who had not a bed to offer him. He had made himself poor, was he not entitled to some of the proceeds of what was given to the poor to alleviate his own hardships? My experiences as a prison chaplain showed me it was an almost invariable rule that prisoners made excuses for themselves and even when they admitted their guilt, extenuated it. This makes one believe that Judas may well have " rationalised " his actions in some such way. At any rate, it is easy to see that his zeal in regard to the box of ointment, which should have been sold for the poor, was, as St. John thinks, a cover for his sin.

It is wholly in accord with the character of wrongdoing that one sin leads to the necessity of another. Like the novice playing chess against a strong player, one weak move ties the hands and demands other moves in consequence which would never have been made of choice, till the inevitable checkmate ensues. So Judas began with pride, pride which the Middle Ages rightly counted among the seven deadly sins,

and went on to lose the sense of fellowship, to thieve, and then to cover his
theft with hypocrisy. The result was
a perished conscience. Peter, at a look
from his Lord, went out heartbroken.
Judas, as Jesus looked at him, went
out to betray Him.

The psychologist must regard the
story of Judas as one of conflict and
repression. It was altogether inevitable.
Judas lived in the company of Jesus,
hearing His words, outwardly serving
Him, yet all the while was morally
rotting. No man, not even a Judas,
could remain unimpressed by the personality of his Master. To know Him
as Judas did meant either to love or
to hate Him, there was no middle way.
Judas was living in two atmospheres,
trying to react to two sets of conditions,
the one made by the presence and
teaching of Jesus, the other by his
own moral deterioration. The result
of such a conflict was unconscious repression and with it, misery.

The uneasy conscience of Judas would misread everything and apply to his own case whatever Jesus said. Perhaps he was tortured by doubts as to how much the Master knew or suspected of him. He imagined he was being " preached at." This roused in him a furious counter reaction, an attempt at all costs to justify himself to himself, a process which is far more important than most of us recognise. Instead of settling the conflict by confession and repentance, he began, no doubt unwittingly, to project his own sense of reproach on Jesus, just as he had previously projected the sense of his isolation, which was the result of his own feelings of superiority, on the supposed aloofness of his comrades.

Here we reach the true reason for the betrayal. To set it down as a mere desire for thirty pieces of silver is a strange misreading of all psychological probabilities. We might assume that Judas had become for unknown reasons

so desperately anxious to save himself
from some blackmail or impending ruin,
that he snatched at the chance of the
money which the betrayal would offer
him. This assumption, however, is supported by no evidence, and it is much
better to conclude that the desperation
caused by the repression to which he
had been driven, took the form of
a violent reaction against his Master.
The fact that he hurled the money
back is evidence of such a change as
would come when the act of vengeance
had been satisfied and the reaction set
in. If his motive was mere coarse
covetousness, such a deed would be
much less likely. There seems no
reasonable ground for doubt that Judas
projected his own wretchedness upon
his Lord in one fierce act of un-
controllable hate.

Needless to say that his anger was
baseless. To look for a rational motive
in such complexes is beside the point.
The Master had washed his feet in

touching humility, but Judas was untouched. He had given him the sop at the Last Supper, and Judas had seized it with frenzy, leapt from the room and disappeared into the night. Not one word of reproach had been spoken. The others were totally unaware till the very last who the traitor was. They even asked " Is it I ? " Stronger proof than this of the imaginary character of Judas's grievance cannot be afforded. Not covetousness, not well-grounded wrath, but the frenzy of a man half beside himself with the misery he did not know was the result of his unconscious conflict, sent Judas out to the priests.

When he came with his rabble into the garden, his hatred had grown cool and cunning. He determined to dissimulate it with a kiss. This was not merely a sign. He gloated over the surprise he would give the One he hated. Jesus should receive the kiss, and, before He knew it, find Himself a prisoner. Then Judas would be well avenged. Then he would laugh in triumph. The scheme went well. The words with which he was greeted were amazing. "Friend" not traitor. Only Jesus could say that. However, Judas had changed, Jesus had not changed.

Dr. Rendel Harris has made a fascinating suggestion. On a first century cup of common pattern he found an inscription of which the first words are identical with these—"Friend, why art thou come hither?" They add, "Be merry." The inscription was obviously meant as an invitation to drink after the manner of the legends we have round some kinds of pottery to-day which invite us to another cup. Most of us think of the cup used at the Last Supper as a noble chalice, a "Holy Grail." But the house of the man who was the host was not likely to provide such for his poor guests, and it is much more probable that the cup was a common bit of pottery like the cup Dr. Harris mentions. It may have had an identical inscription. If so the words used by Jesus may have been a last appeal, reminding Judas of the cup from which he had just partaken. In any case, they were in vain. The only other words spoken were a pathetically noble reproach. " Betrayest thou the Son of Man with a kiss ? " Judas perhaps realized at that moment for the first time that Jesus had known all the while. He disappears from the scene until the last act of the tragedy.

What seemed so incredible at first is gradually becoming clearer. Judas hated Christ because he hated himself. He projected his own conflict and misery on Him. He had become morally insane, and psychology recognizes moral madness just as much as the more familiar intellectual insanity. I recollect a tragedy of a type not uncommon. A village lad loved the village coquette, who played with the surge of his adolescent sex sense, drawing near and then coolly and laughingly withdrawing, smiling him to frenzy, and then chilling his heated fervour by a display of pouts and frowns. At last the lad, in a fit of sadistic madness, throttled her in the field, and ran away to the village policeman. Leading him to where the poor clay lay, he fell beside the body in an agony of grief, screaming that he had done it because he loved her so. Psychology is the last adviser law seeks; wilful murder was the jury's finding, and the wretched lad went, let us hope, to find something of the mercy of Him who knoweth our frame and remembereth that we are dust. But the despair of Judas was close kin to that. In the awful revulsion of feeling that followed when the blow had been struck, he went in pitifully vain endeavour to his accomplices as if he imagined they would feel as he did. " I have sinned," he sobbed, " in that I have betrayed innocent blood." The poor wretch got cold comfort. "That is your affair" they sneered, and Judas realized at last that the last hope was gone. For the first time the full enormity of his deed came over him. Even then he might have knelt at the foot of the Cross, and would surely have heard the words, "Father forgive him. He knew not what he did."

The suicide of Judas was an act of sheer despair. His state of mind impelled him to do something. Activity is the only alternative to madness in such cases. He found no place for repentance. He dare not face men. He dare not face himself. He decided to face his Maker. With Him we must leave Judas. The judgment of Dante placed him in the lowest hell, but the judgment of Jesus, who knew what was in man, would surely have been more merciful.

The story of Judas shows that even the influence of Jesus, constantly and personally applied, cannot save a man who makes no response. But Judas did respond. It was the presence of Jesus that created the conflict in his heart. Just as air means life to the living and decay to the dead, so the presence of Jesus, which gives life to the living soul, hastened the moral decay of Judas. It is possible to be an apostle and an apostate at once.

Indeed, those who know Jesus as Judas did must either love or hate Him. Perhaps that is why when a Christian falls, his fall is often so utter. Really to know Jesus makes it impossible to be indifferent to Him. We must either love or hate Him. Judas hated Christ, because he hated himself. He projected his own conflict upon his Master and struck at him the blow he owed to himself. The first sin for which Christ suffered on the Cross was the sin of the man who betrayed Him there,—" Such gainsaying of sinners against themselves."

The story of Judas shows that salvation is no automatic process by which Christ permeates a life. It shows, too, that environment cannot make character. It stops the hasty judgment that we make when someone brought up in a Christian home fails utterly in the day of trial, and we say there must have been something wrong in their upbringing. What was wrong in the environment of Judas, save himself?

Salvation is, therefore, no matter of environment. Judas, in the very presence of living salvation, goes unsaved to his doom. That presence hastened the process of his downfall. The miserable traitor in the limelight of shame stands out to tell all time that although Christ may be in the life, if He is not in the heart there is no salvation. In the life of the penitent thief Christ had no place, but on the Cross, by His side, suffering broke through the hardness of his heart and he received salvation. His case was the direct opposite to that of Judas. Together, the two point out how Jesus saved and how He failed to save.

In the desire to glorify God, theology has often assumed the work of salvation to be entirely divine. The work may be, but the response that makes the work effective is human, and not even the power of Christ can make that response for the man who will not make it for himself. Christ saves where man will let Him save. Judas shows us where the plan of salvation breaks against the rock of man's own evil. There is no evidence to call Judas a moral monster. His case is that of many. It illustrates the danger of coming into contact with the purity of Jesus which is a consuming fire to burn those it does not cleanse. Jung's celebrated theory that Paul was a Christian when he was a persecutor, persecuting himself in his persecution of others, fighting against the Galilean who had already conquered him, is more true than many of the views of psycho-analysts about religion. Judas illustrates the same law. He hated himself and struck at his Master in consequence. " Good were it for that man if he had never been born "—it is better never to know of salvation than to know and then refuse.

VIII

THE OLD TESTAMENT AND SALVATION

IN Mr. H. G. Wells's fascinating book, "Kipps," one meets the prosperous proprietor of the drapery emporium where Arthur Kipps serves his apprenticeship. He is Mr. Edwin Shalford, who goes through life with two mottoes, " 'Fishency " and " System." His philosophy of life is to hustle and save. " Even his religion," says Mr. Wells, " was to save his soul."

The redoubtable Mr. Shalford is not the only man who by his religion has sought to save his soul, and, in seeking to save, has lost it, forgetting that salvation is a gift of God rather than an attainment of man. Yet this gift is not realised, as we have already seen, without certain conditions being fulfilled on the part of man, and the history of religion is very largely the story of a quest to discover and fulfil them. Man has sought salvation ever since

he has been religious, and although
our own ideas of salvation have come
to us mainly in the thought forms of
Judaism, the ideal of salvation has also
been the centre of the religious thought
of many nations. We must remember,
as Dr. Anderson Scott points out in
his interesting book, " Christianity According to St. Paul," that the question
" What must I do to be saved ? " came
as readily from the Greek gaoler of
Philippi as from any Jew acquainted
with the Old Testament.

This question, " What must I do to
be saved ? " was not merely asked some
nineteen hundred years ago by a Greek :
it is the plaintive demand of the world
to-day. The previous chapters lead
us to say that the same answer is
all-sufficient now as then—" Believe
on the Lord Jesus Christ and thou
shalt be saved." A simple statement,
no doubt, yet involving the greatest
issues of life — what is meant by
" believing " on the Lord Jesus Christ,

and what is implied by the idea of salvation? It is not the place here to discuss the implications of belief in Christ. This great fact of experience has been treated, from time to time, mainly from the psychological point of view, in other chapters. Rather is it the purpose of this chapter to discuss historically man's developing ideas of the nature of salvation. The climax naturally comes with the revelation of Christ as Saviour. Yet long centuries passed before this " fullness of time " gave to the world her greatest gift, and no satisfactory account can be given of what the New Testament means for our salvation until we consider how the way was prepared by the seers and prophets of Israel.

The Old Testament has been well called the history of a salvation, and the Fourth Gospel puts this in another way in recognising " Salvation is of the Jews." Indeed, the creed of Israel was " Jehovah saves," and the Old

Testament is the record of the proving of this belief through many centuries of adventure. The general fact of a salvation remained unaltered through all the years; it is in the concept of that from which man is saved that we trace development. It is, moreover, only as God gives light that man realizes the darkness from which he is saved.

In the Old Testament, emphasis is chiefly placed upon what may be called the "negative" rather than the "positive" aspect of salvation. In other words, deliverance from danger and evil claims more immediate notice than the possession of blessings. In the early days of Israel, moreover, the conception of salvation was national and political. Much water had to flow under the bridge before the vital and personal aspect came to the foreground, and salvation could be the comprehensive term for all the values of the Christian Gospel, the bestowal of "every spiritual blessing."

It is a hard truth that so many in the great religious history of Israel never discovered what salvation meant. Though the word itself is of most frequent occurrence in the Old Testament, a great number of the references are unworthy of their subject. Some scholars maintain that the greater part of Israel never discovered a nobler salvation in Jehovah than Moab found in its god Chemosh. This, however, applies to the " political " rather than the " spiritual " Israel, for there was always a " remnant " in which lay the true heart of religion. The " chosen people" are thus really those in Israel who themselves chose to discover the moral will of God, and who proved in their own experience, by doing that will, what God's salvation meant. Inasmuch as they were willing to respond to the guidance of God, the legacy of a lofty conception of salvation is inherited from them. A large section of the people, however, were content

with an idea of salvation as mere external
deliverance from harm. Indeed, through
many periods of religious history salvation
and deliverance were regarded as practically synonymous. Thus the Hebrew
word generally translated by the Revised
Version of the Old Testament as " to
save " can in a large number of cases
be rendered " to deliver " or " rescue."
To draw a dividing line, however, between
material and spiritual deliverance would
be very difficult, and alongside of many
passages which would normally be interpreted on material lines we must
allow the possibility of a spiritual
interpretation.

The Book of Judges, which tells
the story not so much of " judges "
in the modern sense of the word as
of " mighty men of valour " on behalf
of their nation, is a record of men's
early ideas of salvation. Thus we read
that God sent Gideon " to save Israel,"
and the salvation he works is one of
success in battle. So, too, Othniel,

the conqueror of the King of Meso-
potamia, is described as a " saviour "
or " deliverer." Small as this conception
of salvation may seem, one outstanding
truth here presents itself—God alone
brings salvation ; the " judges " are
instruments He chooses to effect His
purpose.

This aspect of a material salvation
also appears in much later literature,
especially the Psalms. It is not absent, as
we shall see, in the New Testament, which
fact suggests that spiritual values are
intimately related to material conditions,
yet of course, they are not dependent
on them. But occasionally in the Psalter
we get somewhat crude statements of
their relationship. Thus the Psalmist
prays " Save now, we beseech Thee,
O Jehovah, send now prosperity." Such
a desire is consonant with the prevalent
Hebrew conception that prosperity was
the reward of the good and religious,
and disaster that of the ungodly.
This became true in so far as men

realised that the only true way of life was God's way, yet the lesson of the Exile, and in due time, the lesson of the Cross itself, as we have been reminded in Chapter ii, taught that God's way of life for men might be to tread the path of suffering. The passage from the Psalms quoted above should not be understood as representative of all others. A very different and spiritual aspect is evident in such words as " Lead me in Thy truth, and teach me ; for Thou art the God of my salvation, on Thee do I wait all day."

Salvation in the Old Testament has meaning chiefly for *this* life. The after-world of the Hebrews, that vague and shadowy " Sheol," was not a place in which salvation might be expected. Only in the later literature, such as the Book of Job, is the hope born that God will deliver after this body is gone to dust, for there is always One who is alive to vindicate the just. In spite of this external view of salvation on the part of early Israel, however, it was brought to bear that necessary spiritual conditions were involved. Chief among them was moral obedience to the will of God. Thus it was taught that any calamity which threatened the nation could be averted by the people's return to righteousness.

It will already have been evident that salvation in Israel was both national and individual. The former, however, was the more characteristic in the thought of her people. " Salvation is of the Jews " as a nation because Israel revealed to mankind that social salvation is the greatest implication of the individual. The Jewish ideal for mankind was to be realised in a social organism. Jehovah had not merely chosen certain men, but had also called a people to be His in an especial way, to express in national as well as personal relationships the salvation which was His gift. It has thus been said that the conception of a social salvation is the contribution *par excellence* of pre-exilic Israel to the spiritual progress of the race. This is no mean contribution, and many have thus been led to realize that God has no blessing for the individual apart from what He offers to all His children, that salvation can only be worked out in the service of others.

That Jehovah would save His people was to the Jew guaranteed by His first great saving act in delivering Israel from Egypt. This was, in a large measure, regarded as a presage of His future favour to the nation. Non-Jewish historians might fail to see in the narrative of the Exodus what is evident to the interpreting eyes of the Israelite. But nothing can detract from its deepest significance, as a foretaste and guarantee of salvation, to the Jewish people. The deliverance effected by God through the Exodus meant that Israel had been chosen as the pre-figurement of a redeemed humanity. That this was foreseen in early days is indeed a matter of wonder.

The prophets who show us the morally corrupt condition of the nation were, in many cases, bold to predict a true salvation born of Israel. It appears that the very darkness of despair gave birth to the highest vision of salvation; the gloomiest days may suggest the brightest. Isaiah, himself conscious of sin, and living amongst "a people of unclean lips," in days when religion was mere profession and worship an offence to God, prophesies that even from the city which is the centre of corruption shall come forth righteousness and truth for all the world. Dr. John Oman has reminded us that we find this vision in the teaching of Jesus Himself. The religion of the then-best people in the whole land is decried as mere formalism, yet St. Luke records that Jesus declares that the kingdom of God is in the midst of them.

The exile brought about a vast transition in Jewish thought on salvation. We must now recognize that those years of intense anguish and suffering, when all seemed lost, were in reality the birth pangs of a glorious new life. It was found that the salvation God was purposing for Israel was a thing infinitely greater than material values; it was the relationship of the human soul to God. Where God dwells, there is salvation. It was realized too that God's presence was not conditioned according to the well-being of the nation, but that He was everywhere, in all circumstances even of the exile, to be apprehended by every man of pure heart and mind. Salvation still had social implications, of course, but its hope was now greater than a national claim upon God; it rested upon a personal covenant with Him. Thus we find that salvation becomes chiefly a matter of the experience of individuals. The post-exilic prophets make this emphasis, and Jeremiah, with his experience of the exile, leads the way. The covenant he proclaims is no mere national contract between Jehovah and Israel: it is a covenant of the heart, made with each and every individual who will respond —" I will put my law in their inward parts and in their heart will I write it . . . they shall all know me, from the least of them unto the greatest of them, saith the Lord, and I will forgive them iniquity, and their sin will I remember no more."

Though this is a new covenant, we note that the author of salvation is still the same. It is God who alone will save His people : Israel had learned this great fact that there was none other. She had sometimes looked to other nations and powers to save her, but had found it was in vain—" in our watching we have watched for a nation that could not save." Trust had been falsely placed in princes and the sons of men in whom there was no help. Just as Israel realized there was but one God, so too, was she convinced that there was one Saviour, and that " salvation belongeth unto the Lord."

As the idea of an individualistic covenant gained ground, there followed almost of necessity the corollary of a doctrine of resurrection. It came gradually, but made itself increasingly felt, for men realized that if God cared for and extended his salvation to each individual, He would not allow His saved ones to perish in the dust. Salvation would, therefore, be consummated in the future. On the national side, the idea of a consummated salvation took chief expression in the hope of the Messianic kingdom. The expectation of this dominates a great portion of the post-exilic literature. Israel believed that there must be a joyous conclusion to all the trials of the exile, and a " happy ending " to the most pessimistic writings of her prophets. It would, at length, be God's good pleasure to favour His people and set up a reign of peace and prosperity in their midst. The then-present condition of things was bad, but since God was Almighty and All-wise, the future must redeem the present.

The climax of the prophetical message is expressed in this great hope of the founding, through and after the suffering of Israel, of a universal rule of peace and justice. Also, since it was God alone who could save, He, too, would bring this glorious reign of His into being. The hope was not that the Messiah would inaugurate this new age of salvation. God would bring in the kingdom, and the Messiah would be His chief representative in and over it. It would seem that the Jews did not concern themselves especially with regard to the actual way in which the new age would come. The manner of its inception was of secondary importance : of real account was that the promised salvation would surely come from Jehovah Himself, and would be a day of His victory and triumph.

Though the new age would come about through travail and anguish, it is very doubtful whether the Old Testament ever speaks of a suffering Messiah. The disciples of Jesus themselves later thought it impossible that suffering should be the lot of their Messianic King. Thus the Old Testament pictures Him as a man of royal dignity and birth, a "Son of David," who would pronounce judgment to all the nations which would ultimately form the glorious kingdom of Jehovah. Some writers, however, foretold that the Messianic kingdom would be for Jews alone; they would administer God's salvation to the nations. But the greater vision, which is so beautifully expressed in such books as Micah and "Second" Isaiah, finds no room for Israel's political supremacy. All nations should come into God's new kingdom of the saved, and be His. Thus Jerusalem would be the scene not merely of universal dominion, but of universal worship. Great as this vision was, however, it never reached the heights which Paul saw when he preached that all national distinctions could be completely lost in the higher unity of God's kingdom —" where there cannot be Greek and Jew, circumcision and uncircumcision, barbarian, Scythian, bondsman, freeman." Yet the salvation of the Messianic kingdom would be a means of blessing for many peoples ; it would bring not victory in war, but peace on earth. In the beautiful passage where Zechariah pictures the Messianic king entering his city, he is portrayed not as one who proudly rides a horse, the symbol of militarism, but who meekly strides an ass, the symbol of peace, trade, and friendly international relations. He is " just and having salvation," and the salvation thus ascribed to him is comprehensive of all the blessings of the new age, even as salvation in the New Testament, as we shall see, implies the whole fruit of the Gospel. This, incidentally, is a side-light that serves to show the unity and continuity throughout the ages of man's idea of salvation.

N

We have already seen that, though the essence of realised salvation was conceived to be a life of individual communion with God, a life which was just the possession of individuals alone would not suffice. The experience was individual, yet, of necessity, social also. Eventually a redeemed society would be its goal, and the greatest redeemed society was a redeemed world. The Messianic hope had pointed to this, yet had stopped short in that its nature was a kingdom of this world, wherein God's glory cannot be fully contained. It would eventually be manifest not in things man-made, but God-made. A revelation of a kingdom entirely God's must come—this is the essence of what is called "apocalyptic." The Messianic and apocalyptic hopes are in many aspects one, yet the latter goes further in its expectation of a definite divine intervention into the affairs of man, so that the earthly is changed for the heavenly, and salvation becomes a complete revelation of God who is "all in all." This final salvation, it was thought, would follow the destruction of the present evil world. Some of the later Jewish books picture the Messianic kingdom as also belonging to this world to come, and consider the salvation to be experienced then as the only salvation that will ever be fully realized. The importance of this apocalyptic hope of salvation can hardly be over-estimated in considering the biblical evidence. It played no small part in the mind of our Lord Himself as did also, of course, the Messianic hope. Though Jesus definitely applied the latter to Himself, and also spoke frequently in apocalyptic terms, it is consonant with His genius for using the best only of the Scriptures that He found no place for the fantastic conceptions that ran riot in later Jewish literature. In the Book of Enoch we read, for example, that the new age of the "saved" humanity would be one in which the world of nature tries its utmost to supply the redeemed with every material blessing. The privilege of the righteous will be each to beget one hundred children, whilst every measure of olives will yield ten presses of oil!

There was, indeed, a real danger lest the greater, spiritual vision of salvation should lose its " other-worldliness " in a materialistic outlook. Undoubtedly the period just described was in most respects one of retrogression, and another powerful influence that then endangered salvation in terms of the spirit was the setting up of a ceremonial law. To obey such a law became for many the making of a sure claim for salvation. A similar danger has been constant throughout many ages : all too often has the Church been guilty of meting out salvation according to man's obedience to a code. Yet religious law does not, surely, necessitate this, for its pre-supposition is grace. The charge of

" legalism " as such could not, moreover, be raised even against Ezekiel, who, above all, gave Israel her later systematised law code. Yet Israel, fettered as she found herself by bondage to her law code, found no ultimate salvation of the grace of God. For centuries the chains of the law held her down, and it was to a fettered Israel that Paul proclaimed Christ as the breaking of that bondage.

Looking back on Israel's quest for salvation, it is clear that she had dreamed a great dream of the inexhaustible riches of God, yet a legal and material hand had bound her so strongly that she never awakened in freedom. The way was prepared, but salvation was still in the future.

*From the Standpoint
of the Bible*

IX

THE NEW TESTAMENT AND SALVATION

THE NEW TESTAMENT AND SALVATION

AS we read the New Testament a new world of saving powers swims into our ken. " Thou shalt call His name Jesus, for He shall save His people from their sins "—so St. Matthew reminds us that the very name Jesus means " Saviour." As He went about His ministry men began to discover that not only did He bring salvation, but that He *was* salvation in His own Person. This is no mere metaphor. He was, and is, that perfect oneness of God with man and man with God which *is* salvation. Israel had found that communion with God was salvation : in Jesus Christ this communion was perfectly realised. Thus when He came to the home of Zacchæus it is recorded that Jesus Himself says " This day is Salvation come to this house." Our Lord's early followers, however, never fully grasped the truth of this, in so much as they never paid Him Divine honours. Salvation was God's, and although they gradually realised that Jesus was becoming the means of it in their own lives, their essential Jewish monotheism prevented them going further. The realisation that He did not merely reveal attributes of God, but the whole of God's saving love, was a long way ahead. The Cross was eventually to shew this. The fact that only once do the Synoptic Gospels call Christ " Saviour " points to the conclusion that it was chiefly after His death that men began to comprehend the fuller meaning of His saving work. They found that Christ had taught no theory of God's saving love : He was Himself the expression of it.

It has been shown that in the Old Testament salvation frequently implied deliverance from physical ills. An outstanding advance that the New Testament makes is in its insistence on salvation as spiritual deliverance. There are, of course, a considerable number of New Testament references where the word "to save" implies the healing of illness, escape from disaster, or deliverance from death. Yet these affinities with Old Testament conceptions are to be expected. The disciples of Jesus were far from founding a new religion; they were endeavouring to express a fresh experience. Their religion was still that of the Old Testament, but with this difference, that through their knowledge of Jesus a new light had come—"the shining morning face of the young church." They realised that the power of God to save was working in their Master. This realisation was gradual; the early days of Christ's ministry meant no "mass movement." They simply record His going about, doing good and making personal contacts with people whose need was sometimes spiritual, sometimes physical. Although the salvation He brought was to find its fullest demonstration in the future, it was an immediate experience also, a foretaste of God's saving power through all life. Salvation was already effective in Him, because in Him the Father's power was supreme. Thus the miracles of Jesus are proof that the world is already under God's control—they are signs of actual approach of the kingdom, and must be interpreted from no merely philanthropic or medical point of view, but as having deep religious significance. Jesus taught that love was at the heart of God's universe, and where such love is, the pain of man is God's pain also. His message is not that suffering will be abolished, but that the experience of pain is divine, and, being taken up into the great work of redemption, may be transformed, as it was on the Cross.

All the while Christ's work of salvation was not His own, though, paradoxical as it may seem, He was Himself salvation. We have seen that the Old Testament writers claim God alone as Saviour; the New Testament does not contest this. Christ is Saviour, but only, for want of a better term, as God's "representative." Since He, however, alone perfectly reveals the saving power of God, He is its one mediator to men —"in none other is there salvation: for neither is there any other name under heaven that is given among men, wherein we must be saved."

That men were in need of salvation is axiomatic to Jesus. He did not hesitate to use strong terms to express the condition of men alienated from God. Thus His use of such words as "lost" and "dead" to describe their condition, and their salvation was not least the purpose of the incarnation —"The Son of Man came to seek and to save that which was lost." Equally suggestive are the words expressing the joy of the Father when the "lost" one returns: "this thy brother was dead and is alive again, and was lost and is found." Man's sin that alone can make such estrangement from the

Father, as the Prodigal's, possible, was accepted by Jesus as a fact about which He offers no theory. He never argues about Adam's transgression, or the origin of sin. He knows sin to be real in the world, and entreats men to seek and receive forgiveness and be saved from sin. This He does by showing how measureless is the forgiving love of His Father in heaven. Although His primary mission is that "the lost sheep of the House of Israel" should be gathered into the fold, yet His will was that none should perish, and there were many of His flock outside the small fold of Israel. Indeed, when Paul describes God's saving purpose in Christ, he realised it extended not only to mankind, but affected the universe itself, and it was God's plan "to sum up all things in Christ," for "the whole creation groaneth and travaileth together to be delivered."

The salvation brought by Christ was primarily salvation from sin, not as a legal status, but as a severance of man's fellowship with God. It has often been mistakenly thought that this " reconciliation " came about through Christ's influencing the mind of God and persuading Him to forgive men their trespasses which He formerly intended to punish. Nothing could be further from the truth. Christ, by laying bare the heart of God, shows how God's whole purpose is to save, and His work is really the fulfilment of the desire of the Father's love. Men believed that God must be hostile because of their sins. In this way they felt themselves alienated from Him. Christ, by showing the true nature of God's love, made men feel how ignorant they had been of God's forgiveness. Thus it is that those who think they can never be saved, the " lost " ones, may realise through Christ that they are precious in the sight of God, Who desires their salvation. Many of those amongst whom Jesus moved, however, believed that

there was a way of saving themselves
from sin by keeping the law in all its
minuteness. Not only did they fail
to do this, but the law exaggerated their
consciousness of sin. Although Jesus
Himself never used the phrase
" justification by faith," this was in
effect His message to such men. By
believing in Him as God's revelation,
those who were " weary and heavy
laden " with the yoke of the law might
find their feet no longer on the road
that led to despair, but on the path
of life eternal. When Paul preached
salvation by faith in Christ he preached
the Gospel of his Master. The Apostle
was in his day fighting a battle with
the Judaizers. It is because he meets
them on their own ground that he is
forced to use such terms as " justification
by faith " that do not sound attractive
in modern speech. He is using the
language of the law court to combat
legalism. The legalists said that a man
could be saved only by obeying the

law. Paul knows this is wrong. Rather, says Paul, does man's salvation depend upon his faith in Jesus Christ, which means the will to do God's will. Thus the term " justification by faith " has been well described as " God's acceptance of the will for the deed." St. Augustine summed it up when he said that God accepts mankind " not for what we are, but for what we may be."

As Jesus lived amongst men, the very power of His personality that drew out their trust for Him brought a realization of their potentialities, all that they might be. Their lives became different spiritually, and often physically also. Both the spiritual and the physical, moreover, were different yet complementary aspects of the one saving " kingdom-power " exercised by Jesus —" thy sins be forgiven thee, arise, take up thy bed and walk." The miracles in the physical sphere are, too, signs of corresponding changes in the spiritual. Jesus opens the eyes of the

o

mind as He heals the physically blind, and He gives life of the spirit even as He restores breath to Lazarus. Faith in Jesus is the one necessity to show the meaning of an otherwise material salvation. So then does Jesus say " Thy faith hath saved thee " with equal reference to both spiritual and material deliverance. He addresses the same words to the woman who anointed His feet in the house of Simon the leper, as to her who sought the stoppage of an issue of blood. The one received spiritual, and the other physical, deliverance. Thus it is the faith entrusted in Him which is indicative of the spiritual meaning of salvation of every kind.

Such faith in Jesus must have been a very natural thing, differing little, in many cases, from personal trust. This is psychologically probable. But as men learned to put personal trust and confidence in Jesus, they thereby began to trust the Father, even though unconsciously. In this way we cannot

separate faith in God and faith in Jesus.
When the storm came whilst they were
on the lake, Jesus rebuked the disciples
for their little faith in His own Person
being surety of their being saved from
drowning. Faith in Jesus, in all things,
was a necessary pre-requisite to the
exercise of God's saving power. Because
of men's unbelief in Himself, in one
place Jesus could do no mighty work.
To have faith in Jesus was thus to
prepare the way for God to save. Such
faith did not look for proof, because
proof was unnecessary. It is like the
faith of a child, content to lie on its
mother's lap, perhaps not understanding,
yet somehow knowing that love is there,
having found nought else. Such, too,
is the faith we have in those who are
really our friends, asking no guarantee
of their faithfulness, never dreaming it
necessary. Once that kind of faith
was there, Jesus could enter men's lives
to save.

" For us men and for our salvation

Jesus came down to earth," says the Nicene creed. True as this is, it should now be pointed out that the fact recorded here is no theory of salvation. The fact of Christ's mission to save cannot be doubted, but a satisfactory theory of that work has always lain beyond the scope of even the great theologians, who all too often have disagreed about it. Yet the theory is of second-rate importance to the fact. Many people who are most " saved " know least about it theoretically ! A man of few opportunities in life, who has, shall we say, been converted by the " Salvation Army " and found in the place of his old life the splendid radiance of Christ's saving love, might not be able to give any coherent explanation of what had happened, yet would be sure that salvation had indeed become his. If the New Testament writers themselves be examined for one " theory " of salvation, it will prove in vain. They bear witness to the fact of salvation, an experience so

comprehensive that it defies definition.
Du Bose, writing on this point, makes
an interesting comparison between the
fact and theory of salvation and the fact
and theory of gravitation. He suggests
that two scientists might differ greatly
in their ideas of the nature of gravity,
yet both acknowledging the fact of the
existence of gravity as primary they
might equally live under it and use
its benefits.

Many of the greatest things life has
in store for us are given, rather than
attained, and are to be accepted more
than understood. Though salvation may
come through a "working out" on
man's part, it is essentially a gift. It
is the greatest gift that God grants
to those who have aspiration and vision.
The fact of our "working out" our
own salvation does not conflict with
this. Salvation is still God's gift, for
He Himself implants in us both the
willing to do and the ability to accomplish
His will. Salvation is entirely of God,

yet we must so conceive the doctrines of grace, as Dr. Oman has pointed out, that salvation shall not in part be God's gift and in part our own achievement, but at once God's giving and our own achieving, remembering that He works in us both the willing and the doing. Man may not be saved by struggling to make himself righteous, but by the feeling of his need of righteousness, which is God's gift unto salvation.

> " All the fitness He requireth
> Is to feel your need of Him,
> This He gives you . . . "

All our struggling to obtain righteousness springs from lack of faith that God will give it through fellowship with His Son. It is an everyday fact of experience that lives are changed by personal influence rather than by a self-discipline to disagreeable laws, which also are on the side of faithlessness. The greatest saving influence in life is called out when it is realised that a love is extended of which one is not worthy. If this

be so of the love wherewith man loves
his brother, how much the more of
that greater love wherewith God loves
man, shown by the giving up of His
only Son on the Cross?

Fellowship with Jesus Christ, God's
greatest saving power, means a seeking
to do God's will. If we seek this alone
we shall need to bother ourselves little
or not at all about our salvation. We
shall be able to leave that entirely to
God, the doing of His will being the
one object of our care. And, as Dr.
Oman again points out, since it is the will
of God that we shall be saved, our
salvation ceases to be an object for our
personal wills at all. Inasmuch as our
highest good is utterly secure in the
will of God, we can forget ourselves
in doing His will, which always implies
the service of others. In this way,
we " lose " ourselves to find our salvation, which will then cease to be merely
" negative "—a deliverance from evils—
but will become a " positive " means

of self-expression. Salvation then becomes life itself, a life of such a quality that it is " eternal."

Stevenson said that in the Gospels no man is damned for what he does, but for what he doesn't do. In other words, to be saved means not merely to avoid doing certain things, but to do many others, to live a fuller life. Jesus came not just to deliver men from certain sins, but that they might have life and " have it to the full." To be saved is to have a larger vision, a deeper sympathy, a broadened outlook. These are characteristic of all who have real fellowship with Jesus Christ. One cannot read Paul's letters without realising how true this was of him, once under the yoke of the law, but now in a service of perfect freedom, discovering a new life which he can hardly contain within himself. The Christ now lives in him, and all things have been made new. Yet the goal even yet is not reached. Great as the

Apostle's present experience of salvation is, he still presses on, counting himself not already to have obtained what God has for him. All this illustrates how vast was the Apostle's conception of salvation. Every aspect of Paul's life would have to come under the saving power of his Lord.

Paul's conception of salvation, then, embraces past, present and future. Much may seem paradoxical, for he describes in his letters an experience that was complete, yet not complete, sure yet dependent all the while on his relationship to Christ, a fact of the past yet an object of hope for the future. Paul could write to his converts, " By grace have ye been saved through faith," yet they are also " being saved " and must look to the future, for salvation is " nearer to us than when we first believed." From this it is all the more evident that what may be so vast an experience can never be systematised or measured.

Though there are all these elements in the New Testament doctrine of salvation, many scholars have tended to emphasise one, the future, to the practical exclusion of the others. This is done in the name of eschatology. There is no room here to enter this most controversial subject ; it may be stated, however, that the writer believes that eschatological teaching plays a very considerable part in the New Testament. Yet its place may easily be over-emphasized. It has been granted already that Jesus frequently spoke in eschatological language, yet the number of passages that could be collected where He used words that cannot reasonably be interpreted eschatologically is greater. In many cases, however, there is no means of telling whether a present or future reference is intended. It has been argued that the use of such participial phrases as " those who are being saved," which occur several times in New Testament writings, emphasizes both the present and the future. The question of eschatological reference in the doctrine of salvation is, however, of second-rate importance inasmuch as salvation in its greatest and " positive " aspect—" eternal life " —is a conception really indifferent to the terms present and future. In the teaching of Jesus (far more than in the teaching of Paul), we see a definite preference for the ethical rather than the eschatological. One might venture even to suggest that the Pauline conception of salvation is definitely more eschatological than the teaching of Jesus, as we know it, would allow. Paul builds much on the assumption that the whole work of salvation would be consummated at some definite point of time in the near future. His letters to the Thessalonians bear abundant evidence of this, and we find Paul using highly fanciful Jewish apocalyptic language to describe this consummation. Yet the goal of it all, that " we may ever be with the Lord," is a very noble hope, a hope of personal union with Christ who is Himself salvation.

Schweitzer, in his recent book "The Mysticism of the Apostle Paul," writes a brilliant chapter on "Eschatological Redemption." He interprets the death of Christ from the view-point of a substitution for the pre-Messianic tribulation conceived by the Jews as essential before the Messiah could bring in God's reign of salvation. Jesus, says Schweitzer, substitutes his own sufferings for those of the elect who were to inherit the kingdom. He had, therefore, gone up to Jerusalem intent on compelling the rulers to put Him to death, with the hope that God would accept His death as an equivalent for the sufferings of the elect, and He would then be able to bring in His kingdom. Fascinating as this view-point is, one feels that "Christ died for our sins" in a more "natural" way. We are led by Schweitzer to imagine that

Christ's death made God change His mind, and accept His Son's death as a substitute for the sufferings of the righteous. But any view of the Atonement that savours of substitution is at best unsatisfactory. Surely it is more in accordance with the facts to interpret the death of Christ as a laying bare of the heart of God to show the real nature of self-giving love. When men realise that such is God's love towards them, as sinners, then God's great saving power is found at work in their lives. When men realise, too, how much forgiveness costs, sin can never be treated lightly. As Dr. Denney once wrote, " There is no such experience in the relations of human beings as a real forgiveness which is painless, cheap, or easy. There is always passion in it on both sides."

Stevens, in " The Christian Salvation," approaches this fact from another point of view. Had Christ's death been merely a martyrdom, he maintains, surely He would have died as joyously as many another martyr for His name and cause. Instead of this, He dies in great anguish : to argue that physical conditions entirely account for this is not in accordance with the known facts of His life. He dies, praying that those who have crucified Him may be forgiven, yet weighed down by the sins of men that hurt Him beyond endurance point. Indeed, some have maintained that He died of a broken heart ; such was the cost of the love God is offering for our salvation and forgiveness.

Because God's saving power was above all manifest on the Cross, it was the Cross, as we have seen, that became the very centre of the apostolic preaching. " We preach Christ and Him crucified," says Paul ; he had " placarded " Christ on the Cross before the eyes of his converts. Beside the fact of Christ crucified Paul wished to know nothing, for to preach the Cross was to preach Christ and the saving love of God.

The Jesus who physically walked Galilee was gone, but the Cross remained for ever as witness, and to replace the old, actual touch with the Master in the days of His flesh. Equally important is the testimony borne to Christ's resurrection, by the early Church, for without this the message of the Cross was incomplete. The resurrection told of no bare physical fact, but of God victorious, and the bonds of death for ever broken. It meant that God's saving power had not ceased on that first Good Friday, for through the risen Christ God still exerted His saving power. There would now be no fleshly limitations to the saving work of Jesus, and His spiritual Presence would live amongst His followers in a way that would entirely compensate for His physical absence. His spirit is with men not merely in the way that the spirit of any great man lives amongst his followers, but in such an overwhelming, personal sense that Paul could

say " I live, yet not I, Christ Jesus
liveth in me." The great phrase " in
Christ " is another testimony to this
experience which to-day is called
" mystical." Yet there is no need to
associate such experience with abnor-
mality, as is often done. Anyone who
claims fellowship with Jesus Christ is
a " mystic," though he might repudiate
the term. As far as self-identification
through fellowship is possible, so far
is it possible, too, to have " mystical "
experience. Paul claimed " He that is
joined unto the Lord is one spirit,"
and through faith-fellowship with Jesus
the experiences of the life of Jesus
may be repeated, as Dr. Anderson Scott
has put it, in all aspects save the physical.
Thus it was natural for Paul, analyzing
his own feelings on his fellowship with
Jesus, to see in his own experience
certain stages that corresponded both
to burial and to resurrection. He also
spoke of " baptism into the name "
of Jesus, which is yet another way of

expressing the realisation of oneness with Him. Inasmuch as Paul himself had " through faith " died with Christ on the Cross and had risen with Him to newness of life, he partook of a life which was no longer mere physical existence but eternal life. His union with Christ had meant a breaking away from the evil of this world, and an entry into Christ's world : a death to sin, a life in God. This was salvation.

Through Christ's great demonstration of the love of God, men realized that their ideas of their alienation from God could no longer stand. Sin alone could alienate men from God, and Christ had died for sin. Through Christ's " at-one-ment " in us man might have " at-one-ment " with God. This has been made possible only by Christ's complete self-identification with our nature. Paul put this in a bold way when he said, " Him who knew no sin he made to be sin on our behalf." There are times when an exaggeration, as

225

Charles Kingsley well put it, is the
best way of telling the truth. Thus
Paul all but says that God made Christ
a sinful man, yet dare not let the words
fall from his lips. He is wrestling
with words that are all too inadequate
to express the great truth of Christ's
coming in the likeness of sinful men,
" tempted in all points like as we are,
yet without sin." Through our identifi-
cation with this Christ in faith, the
spirit which was in Him becomes our
spirit. In so far, then, as He lives in
us, sin departs. When He completely
dwells in us, sin is gone, and there
is " at-one-ment " with God. This
" at-one-ment " is sometimes described
by the New Testament as "reconciliation,"
a word much misunderstood. Reconciliation, however, means above all, the
removal in us of that which separates
from God, of that which makes salvation
impossible. The removal of sin must
be from where sin is ; sin is not in God,
but in us. The removal must be from

us. The change of attitude that is involved is surely a change of man's attitude to God rather than of God's attitude to man. Thus we see that reconciliation is on our side. Christ's death does not propitiate God for our salvation; in fact, the New Testament is singularly free from all expressions that might suggest such ideas, and in this matter the Christian religion stands especially in contrast with the majority of religious faiths that aim to propitiate the Deity. In view of this, " reconciliation " may perhaps be thought an unfortunate term. It is the best, however, that has been found for this experience of forgiving love. Because, too, it is our own human experience that we describe, our language is anthropomorphic. Such inadequacy must be recognized, yet the experience remains unaffected by the ways in which it is described.

Christ's saving power from sin and disease has for some while been in the foreground of this present discussion, yet not only from sin does He save: His greatest salvation is "positive," the gift of eternal life. But before passing on to this aspect, it must be remembered that on the "negative" side Christ saves from sin and also from every kind of bondage, for His salvation is inclusive of all that enters human experience. The age in which Christ lived was bound by much that fetters the world to-day, yet His saving power has made men free from many bonds which have been long forgotten. The ancient world was especially under the bondage of fear—a bondage from which modern man is but slowly escaping. Fear of evil spirits, fear of death, and terrors of all kinds loomed large. The New Testament bears ample evidence of all this. A large part of the saving work of Christ has been the freeing of mankind from such fears. It is scarcely possible now to realize the domination that the conception of evil spirit-forces had over the minds of men in the first century. Disease, as the Gospels and Acts alone show us, was largely accounted for by theories of demon possession. The ancient world lived in constant fear of the mysterious forces of the unseen.

> " Of Cerberus and blackest midnight born,
>   In Stygian cave forlorn,
>   Midst horrid shrieks and shapes and sights
>   unholy."

Yet it was realized from the very first that Christ was Lord of the spirits : indeed the spirits themselves confessed this. Not only did Jesus cast out evil spirits, but He gave His disciples power to do so, and St. Luke records that they returned to Him filled with surprise that even the devils were subject to them. Not all the spirits of the ancient world were originally thought of as evil, of course ; there comes to mind the famous good " demon," the guide and counsellor of Socrates. Such " good " spirits were few : they are scarcely mentioned in the New Testament.

It is not in the scope of this present chapter to examine these phenomena from a psychological point of view. It is here sufficient to acknowledge the reality of their very great influence on men's minds. Moreover, we seldom realise how intense was Paul's belief in these opposing forces of the spirit world—"For we wrestle not against flesh and blood, but against principalities, against powers, against the rulers of the darkness of this world, against spiritual wickedness in high places." Again he writes, "Even so we, when we were children, were in bondage under the elements of the world." These "elements" are to be interpreted as spirit forces, perhaps connected with the supposed magical powers of certain stellar bodies. Yet Paul had a great message of liberation in Christ, for he is "persuaded that neither death, nor life, nor angels (*i.e.*, evil spirits), nor principalities . . .

shall be able to separate us from the love of God, which is in Christ Jesus our Lord." There was a new realm of the Holy Spirit over against the dominion of the evil spirits, and the Christian message came as light in a great darkness. Missionaries to-day also vouch for the joy that this message brings. Schweitzer, writing of his experiences of missionary work in Africa, has said that, for the negro, Christianity is the light that shines in the night of fear. Men feel themselves cut off from God by evil spirit forces even more than by sin. But the Christian gospel is of a Saviour who " delivered us out of the power of darkness and translated us into the kingdom of the Son of His love." Men do not now talk of Christ's freeing them from demons, though they may put it in a different way and, using modern terminology, say that He delivers from nervous disorders, and complaints that psychology might diagnose as " com-

plexes." Where the love of Christ
reigns, a peace that passes our understanding stands sentry over our lives,
and leaves no place for fear. Thus
he who is at one with God through
fellowship with Christ stands fearless
of all things, because of the knowledge
that not even death can separate from
the love of God.

The world into which Christ came
had no such message. Man had long
demanded an assurance for immortality,
yet none was given. The mystery religions
promised a "salvation" in a future
life, but it was for the few, the fully
initiated, and its basis was but philosophical argument which made no sure
appeal. The words of Catullus echo
the despair of the ancient world :

> *Soles occidere et redire possunt*
> *Nobis cum semel occidit brevis lux*
> *Nox est perpetua una dormienda.*"

(Though suns may set and suns may rise,
When once for us the brief light dies
Night's endless sleep must close our eyes).

In Christ was heard no empty speculation, but the triumphant cry " He is risen." It was the news of salvation for those " who through fear of death were all their lifetime subject to bondage." There comes a day when all death will be " swallowed up in victory." The fact of Christ's resurrection is indeed the only satisfactory account of the existence of the Christian Church ; it to-day remains the very corner-stone of our salvation.

Yet the salvation offered through Christ's resurrection avails for us in no " mechanical " way. Because He broke the bonds of death, it does not follow thereby that all have done so too. Life is granted to us only as we accept it. Our chief hope of immortality is that this life is too small for us to express in it the whole of God's purpose for us. The late Professor Fearon Halliday once suggested that the reason why so many people do not hope for a life to come is because they have nothing in this life really worth conserving and developing. It is the knowledge of a greater love than this existence can express that is man's guarantee of a life to come. Christ has shown not only that the bonds of death can be broken, but that we may have something of such value in this life to assure that it can never be destroyed. This is the essence of His salvation; He offers this greatest gift—" The gift of God is eternal life in Christ Jesus." Eternal life begins here and now : it is so great that death has no dominion over it. Christ then has saved from every enemy of this life, and from that last enemy, death. " Death, where is thy sting, O grave, where is thy victory ? " Nothing is beyond the power of Him Who alone can save, and save " to the uttermost."

" After this I beheld, and lo, a great multitude which no man can number, of all nations and kindreds and people and tongues, stood before the throne

. . . . and cried with a loud voice, saying, Salvation to our God which sitteth upon the throne, and unto the Lamb."

*From the Standpoint
of the Future*

X

A GALILEAN SOCIETY

JESUS came to save the world. How far is the process going on, and in what way? The answer is not very encouraging in some respects. The largest church in Christendom is content simply to get the acceptance of her own dogmas and discipline, convinced that this is the essence of salvation. If so, would Jesus be amongst the saved if He returned to earth, for could we imagine Him accepting and proclaiming these doctrines and enforcing this discipline? If we say we can, we must admit that He will have changed very greatly from the Teacher He once was. One can find plenty of authority in traditions, councils, creeds, for these doctrines, but very little in the Galilean ministry.

The Protestant churches are not so uncompromising in this respect, but evangelical religion is apt to restrict conversion to the type envisaged by its own tenets, whilst the crudities of Fundamentalism savour of the Old Testament system of sacrifice, rather than the teaching of Jesus.

Apart from all this, however, we may doubt whether the church is exactly fitted to do the kind of work we have in mind, which is the definite and systematic attempt to transform society according to the principles of Jesus. There are several reasons for this judgment. The early Christian church started as a crusade, but of necessity became something more than a crusading movement. It developed into the custodian of doctrine and discipline, a great social and moral institution in the world. Just for those reasons, it is not well fitted for pioneer work. It is insufficiently mobile, for like all great institutions, it must needs move slowly, perhaps at the pace of the slowest. To say this is not to blame the church, but to realise that there is a task it is not well fitted to fulfil.

Moreover, by reason of the divisions of organized Christianity there is no society that embraces any and all Christians who believe in the salvation or transformation of society by Christ to be an ideal capable of achievement. No church could start such a society and ask others to join. Her own definitely marked out boundaries would not be crossed by those of other or no creeds. Yet there must be a vast number inside and outside the churches who are alive to the need for religious revival and for the fearless application of the Sermon on the Mount as a solution to our social problems.

The time is surely ripe for such a movement. The old materialism is dead. The old antagonism of " science " and " religion " has vanished. The youth of the last generation, rejoicing in the removal of many ancient " tabus," threw its energies into pleasure seeking. Now

241

Q

there is no longer any ban against pleasure, such as lingered in the Victorian days from the old Puritan strain in the mental make-up of England ; pleasure has lost some of its attractions, and there is a seriousness of outlook amongst thousands of the better educated of our young people. This may find fulfilment in religion, or else will undoubtedly lead, in revulsion, to cynicism and pessimism. The time is at hand, and if the fiery cross were sent out, we should be surprised by the response to the call.

The only practicable way is the establishment of a new society, not a church, which can unite people of every denomination without drawing them away from their own church. No particular church must be allowed any special control over it, however. It must avoid at all costs, developing into another sect. It must aim at doing what no church can do, and leave alone what any church can. Let us call such a movement the Galilean society. That will sufficiently show its character, but pledge it to no one aim.

The essentials of such a society are three. In the first place it must be essentially positive. It must have no rules requiring acceptance of any particular belief, save the belief in Christ as the salvation of humanity. It can tell its members to love God and do as they please, for if the former is realized the latter has no dangers. It must not insist on any church-going, or sacrament, but leave the members to follow the rule of their own church in this respect. The society must not turn its energies into attacking even such unsocial practices as war, gambling, intemperance, because there are already organizations doing this work, and the work of the society we are suggesting must be the positive task of building up the good which will overcome evil. It is easier to

attack evil and persuade oneself that
if one eschews certain forms of evil,
negation is a virtue. If once the
society sets itself out on a campaign
against evils of this kind, it will lose
its own character and special task in
so doing.

We have too many " tabus." Many
of them are directed against things
which are evil and unsocial, but the
trouble is that when we declare war
against such things, we at once mark
off as enemies all who engage in them.
For example, a licensed victualler or
a bookmaker, or a man who habitually
bets ; all realise they have no
place in the great majority of churches,
and therefore, keep outside. Yet some
of these men have hearts that are sound
concerning good, and it seems wrong
that the followers of one who consorted
with similar classes in His own day,
should not allow these men to join
with them in any kind of fellowship.
If the society we are describing can

attract some men of this type, it will do much both for them and through them for their associates who are altogether unreached by the churches. The laxity of the Roman church in these matters scandalizes Protestants, but it remains that Rome is the only church that exerts any spiritual influence on this class of man.

The second essential is a definite ideal, which in this case is the application of the Sermon on the Mount to modern life. There is an unmeasured latent capacity for idealism in human nature. The chief lack of modern England is the lack of an ideal. Where the world is fermenting to-day is where there is an ideal definitely before the minds of men. In Italy, Mussolini represents an ideal, and in Russia there is another even still further removed from what Britons would approve. But the fact remains that whether or not these represent ideals of which we approve, they *are* ideals and are dynamic in their influence. In the East where " swaraj " is the ideal, there is a youth movement that has no parallel in this land.

If our newspapers are any criterion of what interests the British nation, the answer would seem to be sweepstakes, murders and sport. But the newspapers, to order of their proprietors and advertisers, have ceased to try to lead public opinion and are content to minister to its more unintelligent aspects. It is impossible to serve God and Mammon, to have a gigantic circulation and cater for thought.

Yet the capacity for idealism exists, and if a new ideal were set forth, it would attract. But not all. Such a society as we are suggesting cannot hope to be more than a leaven, and indeed should not be. We have let ourselves think that the kingdom of God comes in a mass movement. It never will. We are persuaded that all men will enter alike. It cannot be.

As the Hebrew prophets saw, a "remnant" always brings salvation to the nation. The rest must follow where the few lead. To say this may sound undemocratic, but democracy will not flourish any the better for ignoring plain fact. A few always do what has to be done. The rest follow, and it will ever be so. Salvation will not be accepted by a unanimous vote. If the country is to be Christianized, a small "remnant" will do it. The rest will subsequently accept. The society will not trouble about "increases" year by year.

The third requisite is a definite plan. The psychological effect of a plan is incalculable. Most Englishmen are sceptical about the famous Soviet Five Year Plan, and it is certainly not likely to be fulfilled except in a very partial way. But the effect the scheme has had in strengthening the hold of the present regime is perhaps, rather than the actual effects of the plan, what was originally intended. One feels, however, that the precondition of a spiritual revival in this land is a definite ideal, together with a definite plan for realising it, or some part of it in a certain time.

One may consider the present lessened respect alike for the churches and for Parliament. It is not unfairly said that the old parties in Parliament are held together by patchwork compromises, and their policy is one of expediency. They have no definite aim, but drift along hoping that things will mend, content to patch up to-day's difficulty, and leave the future to chance. The swing over of so many to Labour was largely because the Labour party were thought to have an ideal of a greater social justice, and a plan towards it. Similarly, the reaction against Labour was largely because it was felt that the party had failed to think widely and was the instrument of the great Trade Unions. This is not in any way to endorse or reject any of these opinions. It is merely to point out that there is undeniably a lessened respect for Parliament, that cynical things are freely said about the whole business being a game, and that thousands have ceased to take their politics seriously. This is entirely regrettable, but none the less understandable. The state of affairs will mend only when a new ideal and some definite aim of reaching it captures the imagination of the people. Behind a great deal of the fierce criticism on the one hand, and the indifference on the other, to which Parliament is subjected to-day, lies the disappointment, conscious or unconscious, of people who look for some definite leadership and cannot find it. Men desire to be led far more than we generally admit. The born leader never lacks followers, and never will.

Exactly the same applies to the churches. A great deal of cheap injustice is dealt out to them. They have their function, and their particular work prevents them from being the revolutionary organisations their critics demand. As well expect that the main body of an army can do the work of the scouts and shock troops. The church, as a great institution inclusive of many shades of opinion and of many functions, must necessarily move slowly, and her government must be such as will retain in the one body her various members. There is not the least need for such a society as we are suggesting to overlap, quarrel, or interfere with any church. Indeed, the churches will supply the great majority of its members. It will exist for a purpose that the church cannot well undertake. The churches will remain to fulfil their own purpose, and be aided indirectly by the work such a society attempts.

To these three essential things we may add another, which if not essential, seems to be strongly called for; that is a strict discipline. We have already said that the rules would be the fewest, but the society would need the more therefore to avoid at all costs being sidetracked into movements that have nothing to do with its aim, and equally to avoid any compromise in regard to it. The discipline would be exercised by the majority, and whilst there would be no attempt to enforce penalties or launch anathemas, any member who departed from the aim and spirit of the society would be asked to withdraw, but not as an outcast. The society has decided on the path, and as he chooses his own, it would send him away with a Godspeed to his preference, whilst continuing with its own. Much of the criticism levelled against the churches obtains plausibility because the church tries too hard to keep all its members together. A pioneer society like the one outlined need not do so. It could allow any of its members who do not travel at its pace or in its direction, a free and friendly dismissal.

I cannot pretend to offer a constitution

for the movement I am now suggesting. Its basis would be, I take it, belief in God as Love. That would be the whole of its creed as regards Him. To this it would add the belief that the way of divine love has been manifested through Christ, and that the salvation of man, individual and racial, comes through the application of His teaching in the spirit of His life and death. It would allow its members to think for themselves on all theological issues that may arise out of this, and confine itself to the practical issue of trying to make the New Testament ideal a reality.

Such a society might divide itself into three branches. One would concern the work of Research. This would employ those who lack the practical gift of organisation. It would collect the facts and set them out, draw attention to the abuses that need remedy, supply the sociological statistics and investigation that would be needful to prevent hasty and mistaken generalisations. This side would give scope for the student who could consecrate his intellectual gifts to the cause of the Kingdom.

A second branch would deal with what one does not like to call propaganda or publicity, as these terms are associated with things that have a meaning one wishes to avoid. Let us call it the Manifestation branch. It would have the task of calling attention in every possible way to the aims and ideals of the society, and gaining the ear of the people whose aid must be sought in order to carry out our aims. Here, again, is a chance for those who have the gifts of pen and speech.

The third branch would be the Experimental branch. It would be made up of those who have the gift of practical organisation and service and would conduct such actual work as might serve to test the possibilities of larger experiments and the best practical methods of establishing the ideals of Jesus amongst men. Some central organization would be established to unite the three and keep them in touch with one another.

Such a society or movement would need some storm or shock troops to make an impact on the indifference of the world. As we have just said, it is folly to think that a universal invitation can be given to do work of this type and that anyone and everyone may join and effect it. It will never be so, and never has been so. The idea that such is possible is a kind of hybrid between Universalism in theology and democracy in politics—of no credit to either parent. The " remnant " will be the saving power. The rest will follow as they are led.

It is the lead that counts. There is need of something that will strike the imagination and arouse interest. If a number of young men and women would vow one or more years of their life, before they settle down to its full responsibilities, to entirely unpaid work as storm troops, going about the country in apostolic poverty, waking the conscience of the nation, working under their vow, in strict discipline, until the time promised was fulfilled, they would make a deep appeal to the people of England. It will be said this is impracticable. So is the foreign practice of withdrawing young men at exactly this age for a year of conscripted military service. It is entirely impracticable, but it is done. The service of the Kingdom is not likely to be more easily done.

Such a movement would need to be international. But each country would have to think out its own way of approach. To prevent development unrelated to the work in other countries, it would be needful to have some international council, but general aims sent down from some international organization, in which one shares a third of a delegate, command little enthusiasm and are usually quite beside the point likely to appeal to the individual branch ! The movement would need to be largely self-determining in each country, and the national, as distinct from the international, organization would direct its destinies. Moreover, in so doing, it would be content to initiate and leave the various branches a true right to settle their own way of proceeding. Thus, each might accept its task with a sense of personal responsibility. It would be given to this central organisation to work out the plan on which to proceed, and to form branches throughout the land. Each division would have its own opportunity to formulate the way in which to carry out the immediate task set before it, and would be advised to set about it piecemeal, taking so much and aiming at doing it in a certain time, with the understanding that upon each branch carrying out its share according to plan would depend the chance of the other sections doing so. This is to avoid generalised indefinite and exaggerated aims, and to make all realise that if they do not fulfil their share, the rest will be hindered. Too much independence is a bad thing. Nothing keeps us up to the mark better than to know others are dependent on our doing our part promptly.

The programme would be social and humanitarian. It should embrace some ideals of a reform in ways of dealing with crime, and a definite humanitarian aim as regards animals. It is somewhat of a discredit to Christianity that Buddhism should be more prominent in preaching to men their duty to animals. One cannot believe that Christ would have been indifferent to the sufferings of the lower creation. Here, of course, the need for discipline would be apparent. For example, I am personally interested in the abolition of blood sports, and the humane slaughter of animals intended for food, but I have found myself opposed by those who will have nothing

257

R

to do with my aims in these directions unless I identify myself with the total abolition of vivisection and adopt vegetarianism. These things may come, but no sensible person thinks they are likely to be attained in the present generation. We must learn to take first what can be done first, and trite though this seems, the work of reform is more hindered by ignoring this than by anything else. The practical and possible reform is so often wrecked by those who demand all or nothing. The Galilean society must take first what it can hope to attain, and if the all or nothing people cannot agree to this, they must not be allowed to wreck the possible by the demand for what is as yet impracticable. The policy of the half loaf is the only way to the whole loaf.

I can understand some critic saying that I have set out to discuss what is salvation, and end with a programme of vague humanitarianism. He will declare this is unworthy of what Calvary means. Indeed, I could write a very effective criticism on such lines here and now. But it would proceed upon a complete misunderstanding of what I would achieve. I ask simply whether anyone thinks that people in this country are nearer to Christ than they were a hundred years ago. I should say Yes, but if I were asked in what way, I should say that it is because the gospel of love is now more believed, preached and practised ; not because there are more who are in touch with organized Christianity and work in the church.

This seems incontrovertible by experience, facts and figures. If so, is it not a pity that there is not an attempt to take advantage of the new spirit of love amongst those outside the churches ? A new link could be created between the churches and all those who have Christian sentiments and yet are outside the bounds of organized Christendom. Salvation, we have seen, is a very wide experience. It must not be confused with one aspect, the aspect seen when a man is captured for service in organized Christianity, gives up the self-centred life, passes perhaps through a crisis-experience, and becomes a different man. It means that, but we must not so limit it. It means also the transformation of thought, the transformation of commerce, a new spirit of love amongst men. We can leave to the churches the former work, which they have always done and will continue to do. The Galilean society would aim at doing the other task which is supplementary and auxiliary to that of the church, and in no way antagonistic, but such as the church by reason of its special function is not well fitted to fulfil.

The world is facing to-day a crisis without parallel, a future pregnant with the possibility of the collapse of civilization, or at the very least, of its present order. Nations are demanding industrial and international " security," and in order to gain it, setting up barriers, causing suspicion, and creating ideal conditions for the growth of the seed of war. Nations still seem to think that to beggar their neighbours is the way to their own prosperity. We hear talk about a trade revival that will save the situation, and yet most of it seems on the assumption that trade will revive by each nation being a seller to and not a buyer from others. Possibly, if instead of some of the futile subjects injected into the minds of schoolchildren, the elements of political economy had been taught, we might have been spared some of the " remedies " suggested by our popular press. The fact is we need to be told with the sternness of the Hebrew prophets that our plight is spiritual before it is economic, and that nothing but a revival of faith in God and love for man will help us. To say this is not to attempt to use the present distress as a " judgment of God " for our sins.

It is simply the result of the order of national and international life which we have all followed. That order was never right, but it was practicable until the close of the nineteenth century. Since then it has collapsed utterly, undermined by the new relationships made possible by a century's development of methods of world communication and transport, just as much as by the world war it begat. It is no longer even economically possible that the old isolation and self interest should provide a basis for civilisation in the future. The present civilisation came into being as nations grew from mere aggregates of separate tribes into national unity. Exactly the same process is being repeated on the international scale. But where is the international patriotism that can do for the greater combination, what national patriotism did for the lesser? There is only one *internationale* that is not based on such class or financial interests as must inevitably restrict its scope to the few, and that is the Kingdom of God, which creates in so far as men will accept it, a brotherhood of man based on the Fatherhood of God. The salvation of mankind in the material sense, let alone the spiritual, depends upon the establishment of a new ideal of human relationship, and this in its turn depends upon a new spiritual vision, the vision of the true meaning of the Kingdom of God on earth. It will always be found that from the long range point of view the decisive factor in history is the spiritual factor.

The misleading belief in automatic progress has received a severe shock during the past twenty years. The future of mankind is still in the balance. It may be that humanity will destroy itself. It certainly will if it persists on the old lines. The real hope of the world is not science or education. It is Christ, and the entrance of His spirit into the heart of mankind. A world may go on without limit on the principles of Galilee. It cannot do so upon the compromises of Geneva. The spirit of Nationalism can no longer serve. The day of Internationalism has been forced on us by the shrinkage of the world, and the interlocking of its interests and destinies. But there is no spirit of Internationalism save the spirit of Christ. There is one religion only that has been adaptable to all races, and that is the religion of Jesus. If the world finds Christ, accept His teaching, and moulds itself on His spirit, a new and international civilization will grow full of untold promise. If not, none knows what will happen, but the great probability is that civilization and perhaps the human race, will perish.

It is somewhat pathetic, when one realises the international aspect of salvation, to see how many good, earnest people have no idea that the life and sacrifice of Jesus mean anything other than that which the interpretation of the mid-nineteenth century with its

insistent individualism, put on them.
It is pitiful that the old phrases should
be reiterated to a world that has lost
all sense of their meaning. I read on
the window of a tramcar the other day
the legend, " Are you washed in the
blood of the Lamb ? " No doubt such
words are sacred to those who understand them, but the impression on the
outsider, if any at all were made, would
be slightly unpleasant. Speak as you
will of the " old Gospel," it yet remains
that a way of presenting it to the present
age must be found, and has not yet
been found. May it not be that our
initial mistake is that we persist in
thinking this country ripe for harvest,
when actually the time is that of sowing.
We have allowed a generation to grow
up indifferent to Christ because it does
not know what He stands for, and how
His teaching is bound up with the
whole future of mankind.

When Jesus gave the parable of the
sower, it will be remembered that the

crowd was so enthusiastic that He was forced into a boat for safety that He might teach from that floating pulpit. To the excited disciples, it seemed that the time had come for reaping, a great mass movement for the Messiah. Jesus replied in His parable. It was a time for sowing, and many would prove poor ground for the word. Are we not trying to reap where we have not even strawed ? The watchword for the day is " Prepare ye the way of the Lord." There will be a revival. Every sign shows its possibility, but it will come and go without result unless we are ready to prepare its way by demonstrating to the world what salvation is, and why it needs, and needs desperately to be saved.

What is salvation ? If the reply can be in a phrase, it is the impact of the Divine on the human, and the focus of heaven upon the earth is Christ. Salvation must have many meanings and many methods alike for the individual and the community, but the aspect of salvation that bears on the present world crisis is that neither statesmen nor trade expansion will bring the world out of its troubles. We shall be saved only when the spirit of Jesus enters into our national and international relationships.

It is with a sense of the urgent need that something be done to set up some practical steps towards making salvation a reality to the age in which we live that this book closes with the suggestions of this chapter. They may be impracticable, open to serious criticism, but they may none the less serve to make it clear that to discuss salvation is to do little, unless the discussion opens some practicable method of proclaiming it.

The time is ripe for such an effort. There is a new piety stirring in our universities, which have often been the cradle of religious revival. The enthusiasm of the Oxford and the Cambridge Group Movements has so far been concerned with the personal exploration of religion, and its deepening in the individual. But the same new young zeal can surely pour itself into some such movement as the Galilean society would represent. The world is ready in its perplexities to listen to an evangel of hope, but its destinies are in the hands of elderly statesmen and diplomats, trained in the old ways, unable to leave them, even in view of their manifest failure, and worse than all this is the fact that most of these men do not believe in any other way.

The Galilean society would not be an evangelistic agency. Its work would be to create the conditions under which a new and effective presentation of the Gospel might be made. It would prepare the way, cast up the stones from it, make ready in the desert a highway for our God. Until that is done, preaching, as far as the majority of mankind is concerned, will remain as ineffective as it now is. Yet the new age of faith is much nearer than we in our pessimistic moments imagine. In the most literal sense of the phrase, for God's sake let us do something. There can be no such thing as utter failure, for if we fail, we shall have at least tried. But He will not fail. It is only we who can fail Him. If we are ready, God is readier, and it is for us to start with God to make known to the present age what is salvation.